Raised-Bed and Container Gardening Made Simple

6 Easy Steps for Beginners to Grow Fruit and Vegetables in Your Own Backyard on a Budget

A. A. Doyle

© **Copyright 2022 - All rights reserved.**

The content contained within this book may not be reproduced, duplicated or transmitted without direct written permission from the author or the publisher.

Under no circumstances will any blame or legal responsibility be held against the publisher, or author, for any damages, reparation, or monetary loss due to the information contained within this book, either directly or indirectly.

Legal Notice:

This book is copyright protected. It is only for personal use. You cannot amend, distribute, sell, use, quote or paraphrase any part, or the content within this book, without the consent of the author or publisher.

Disclaimer Notice:

Please note the information contained within this document is for educational and entertainment purposes only. All effort has been executed to present accurate, up to date, reliable, complete information. No warranties of any kind are declared or implied. Readers acknowledge that the author is not engaged in the rendering of legal, financial, medical or professional advice. The content within this book has been derived from various sources. Please consult a licensed professional before attempting any techniques outlined in this book.

By reading this document, the reader agrees that under no circumstances is the author responsible for any losses, direct or indirect, that are incurred as a result of the use of the information contained within this document, including, but not limited to, errors, omissions, or inaccuracies.

Table of Contents

INTRODUCTION 1

CHAPTER 1: WHAT'S SO GOOD ABOUT RAISED-BED GARDENS ANYWAY? 5

    BUT WHY BOTHER? 6
    IT'S ALL LATIN TO ME 6
    BUT WHAT ABOUT... 9
    GRANDMA'S HOMEMADE MEALS 12
    ALL THOSE CHOICES! 13
    IT HAS WHAT IN IT?! 14
    WHAT ARE WE EATING TODAY? 15
    AND THE REST? 16

CHAPTER 2: NOT YET! BEFORE WE BEGIN 19

    STEP 1: IT'S ALL IN THE PREPARATION 19
        Common Mistakes 20
        And Now for Some Good News 28

CHAPTER 3: CAN YOU BUILD IT? YES, YOU CAN 41

    STEP 2: BUILD YOUR OWN RAISED BED (OR BUY IT) 41
        Tools 42
        Wood 42
        Alternative Materials 44
    STEP 3: THE SOIL MIX MASTER 47
        Where to Find Soil 48
        So, What Makes Good Soil? 50

CHAPTER 5: WATER ME, BABY! 65

    STEP 4: WATERING AND IRRIGATION 65
        How to Water 68
        Automated Watering 72
        When to Water 76

Where to Water 77

CHAPTER 6: TIME TO GET DIRTY! 79

STEP 5: PLANTING 79
Indoor Seed Starting 80
Direct Sowing 82
Companion Planting 90

BE MY POLLINATOR! 93

CHAPTER 7: GROWING, GROWING, HARVESTED! 95

STEP 6: MAINTAINING YOUR MONEY-SAVING CROPS 95
Care 96
Next Year 99

CHAPTER 8: BESTIES OR FRENEMIES? WHAT YOU NEED TO KNOW ABOUT BENEFICIAL BUGS AND PESKY PESTS 101

POLLINATION 102
PEST CONTROL 103
Good Insects 103
Best Plants to Attract Good Insects 105

CHAPTER 9: HERB YOUR ENTHUSIASM 117

WHERE TO GROW HERBS 118
HERB GARDENS 119

CHAPTER 10: GROWING GUIDES 123

BASIL 124
BEANS 126
BRASSICAS 128
CAPSICUM 130
CARROTS 132
CELERY 134
CHAMOMILE 136
CITRUS 138

CORIANDER	140
CUCUMBERS	142
FIGS	144
KALE	146
LEEKS	148
LETTUCE	150
MANGOES	152
MINT	154
ONIONS	156
PARSLEY	158
PEAS	160
POTATOES	162
RADISHES	164
SPINACH	166
STRAWBERRIES	167
SWEET POTATOES	169
TOMATOES	171

SOW THE SEEDS FOR SOMEONE ELSE 173

CONCLUSION 175

REFERENCES 179

Introduction

The sweet aroma of summer. Fresh, ripe fruit, succulent berries, and crisp vegetables draw you into the produce section at your local grocers. With your shopping list in one hand and basket in the other, you follow the smell of sweet strawberries and those memories of perfect summer cocktails. As you pass a display of perfect mangoes, you crave a smoothie or some ice cream. And the sweet potatoes over there? How your kids love sweet potato fries.

You pick up a tomato, thinking of making some salsa for the weekend as you scan the price displays. Your stomach turns. With exaggerated care, you put down the perfectly ripe Roma and turn your back on the sweet smells of summer. Fresh food has been priced out of reach. There's got to be a better way to get your two and five that won't break the bank.

Disconsolate, you head for the freezer aisle. Row after row of bland and mushy food is now all you can afford.

We all know just how expensive life has become, especially with a family to feed. And while our food costs may not yet be this extreme, there is no better time than today to lower them, especially if you have a family to feed.

1

And amazingly, anyone can do it. Even you, who claims to have the black thumb of death and can kill any plant they touch. Come with me as I guide you through the entire process, from finding a place to grow, all the way to showing off your incredible, tasty food to your friends and family.

Learn from my mistakes. Yes, some were funny, like accidentally growing hot capsicums instead of sweet and not knowing the difference until my mother-in-law came for dinner.

And others, well, they were less funny, like when I tried to speed up the ripening of my tomatoes by following a website that told me to add vinegar to my water. I had to go to the grocers for tomatoes for the rest of that year.

Ever since I moved out of the heart of the city, leaving behind my life of takeaway meals and coffee on the go, I have struggled to keep the food costs for my family as low as possible. It was not until I discovered gardening, and raised-bed gardening in particular, that I was able to provide my family with healthy, wholesome, fresh fruits and vegetables. Not only did they love them, but I also managed to significantly reduce our food costs. In the words of Charlie Sheen, "Winning!"

I will grudgingly admit, in hushed tones, that sometimes I do miss takeaway lunches and fancy restaurants. But life has changed, and I am happily settled into suburbia with four hungry bellies to fill every day. Since learning to grow fresh fruit and veggies, our everyday meals have taken on a special meaning. Not only is it healthier, tastier, and cheaper than before, my family and I have the added pleasure of knowing this food was created by our hands, by our work, and by our care and attention.

I can't wait for you to experience the joy of plucking a warm, ripe tomato off the vine, and filling your salad bowl with salad greens you grew yourself. What about creamy guacamole made from your very own avocados?

While the journey is exciting, the rewards? Well, the rewards are life-changing.

Chapter 1:

What's So Good About Raised-Bed Gardens Anyway?

I guess I should start with a definition. I know, kinda boring. But this way we can all speak the same language and have a common understanding as we dive into specifics.

So, what is a raised-bed garden? Odds are you've probably seen them before. What we are talking about here is a raised garden bed constructed, most commonly, from wood, brick, or stone, that contains an amount of dirt.

This could be set into the ground, raised only a few inches from the surrounding soil, or it could be a freestanding open-topped box at any height. I am going to focus on a subset of the latter.

Open-topped containers, both large and small, that are placed at a convenient height for tending plants. These containers could be store-bought plastic numbers, DIY kits with wood and metal sides, or even masonry, if you have the skill to make them.

But Why Bother?

Raised beds, or containers if they are smaller, give you control. Control over the soil, control over the water, and control over the sun. These are all critical for the growth of your plants. Without enough soil, all your plants' delicate parts will be exposed to the sunshine and the plant will wither. Too much water, and like us, they will drown. Same goes for sunshine; too much sunshine will burn your plants like an air fryer, while not enough will have them looking all pasty and white.

This control comes at a cost, however. Not only do you need to know what to do, which is why you are reading this book after all, but the biggest cost is you need to take responsibility. Yes, responsibility. A big, scary, adult word I know, but trust me, you're ready for this.

It's All Latin to Me

I can hear doubt creeping into your mind. "But I kill all the plants I have ever touched. There is no way I can grow a herb garden or salad greens."

But you can! Trust me. While it appears difficult, all shrouded in those Latin-sounding horticultural phrases—like pomology, olericulture, and floriculture—the reality is quite simple. What you just read translates to fruits and nuts, salad greens, and flowers. Today, we are concerned about olericulture, growing food for you. See how easy it is to learn this?

What else can I clear up for you? In the coming chapters we will learn about making your own raised bed or container, what soil to fill it with, and why you need it, watering, care and harvesting, and storing your bounty.

For now, let me start with some of the more practical benefits. The most obvious one? Raised beds and container gardens look bloody beautiful. Depending on your aesthetic, you can arrange your containers and raised beds in perfect rows down the long axis of your space or radiating out from the fire pit in the centre of the yard or even create a maze, forcing your guests to enjoy the entirety of your garden as they wander. The possibilities are endless, and you are not restricted to growing in the soil of the backyard.

Does your side yard get sunshine? Well, you can put some raised beds on that asphalt, and suddenly you have sweet-smelling basil and rosemary welcoming you to your side yard. What about your driveway, if you happen to live in a place with one? Can you imagine how nice it would be to come home to a series of planters bursting with plump, ripe tomatoes and perfect cucumbers? Pretty sweet idea, isn't it?

By keeping the soil at a convenient, working height, and with you paying so much attention to them, you will be able to maintain a better quality soil. Sounds pretty fantastic, doesn't it? Yes, but the reality is much more pragmatic.

Every time you check on your plants, you will pull out that errant weed, pick out an annoying caterpillar, and just generally look after the soil. Now, this also presents you with a great opportunity to top up the soil around your plants. Soil compacts with rain. The plants will consume portions of the soil, and soon enough your planter, raised bed or container, will be filled with roots and very little soil.

But you can manage that. Every day when you check on your plants, you will notice the changes in the soil. Is it too dry? Too wet? Missing? You can add new soil, or compost if you have some available, and this will add beneficial nutrients and microbes to your planter.

With almost no effort on your part, you are creating and maintaining a no-till garden. And the benefits from that practice will increase your yields the longer you grow.

With raised beds and container gardens, the dirt, and the plants, are raised up to a convenient, working height, as we have already mentioned. Not only does this give you the opportunity to properly care for your plant—as well as save your back and knees from hours of hot torture as you crawl about on all fours pulling weeds—it has the incidental advantage of presenting the plants at the perfect height to enjoy.

When was the last time you really looked at the blossoms on a Thai basil? Or watched a honeybee pollinate an entire tomato plant? How about the journey of a ladybug as it hunts down aphids?

With your plants up where you can see, the curtains will be pulled aside on an entirely new world for you.

But What About…

I know, what about the neighbourhood cats? Yeah, I know they did turn your side garden into a large litter box last season, it is true, but this year you can outsmart them. Cover the old garden with gravel, logs, or recycling bins and grow in a raised bed or a container. Yes, the cats will walk the edge of the raised bed or container, but they are much less inclined to use the dirt as a litter box, especially once the plants fill in.

And before you raise your hands, yes, you can use raised bed and container gardening in a rental. They are temporary by nature. Once you empty out the dirt, disassemble the raised bed, and hose down the driveway, side yard, or back deck, there will be no evidence you were ever there. Obviously, if you put your raised bed or container over the lawn, there might be some dead grass underneath it that you will need to reseed.

But do keep this in mind: Raised beds and container gardens are the ideal solutions for renters, so no you can no longer use that as an excuse to not grow your own food, sorry.

Did I mention weeds? I know I skimmed over how much easier it will be on your knees and back, but what about the actual weeds? I know it will surprise you because it surprised me, but raised beds and container gardens get fewer weeds than growing in the dirt directly.

"But how is this possible?" you ask. It is all about control. When you garden in the dirt, you can amend the soil you have there, but unless you are willing to dig out the entire yard and replace it, you are pretty much stuck with the soil you have. And the weeds that already grow there.

Next time you are bored, look up your house on Google Street View. Shocking, isn't it? All those weeds in the front yard. And just what on earth is going on with the neighbour? Are they setting up a weed farm?

Yep, all those weeds, happily growing for years before you moved in, will have spread their seeds through your backyard. And don't even get me started on that dodgy tradie that poured the oil from his Ute into the dirt against the fence.

You see, you really didn't have a chance. The potential problems with the existing dirt in your yard are too many to count. But now that you are investigating raised beds and containers, you can grow your plants in perfectly moist, nutrient-rich soil. I know you can feel the relief. I can.

And then there is the ease of watering to consider. With the plants happily growing away at a convenient working height, every time you walk by and talk to them, check on them or perhaps sing if you can carry a decent tune, you will notice when they want to be watered. The small leaves may start to curl, or the top of the soil will crumble in your hand. Either way, you can water your charges before they get stressed.

Growing in a raised bed or container garden will also lessen your watering requirements. Combine water-loving plants with other water-loving plants, shade-loving plants with others happy out of the sun, and so on.

The depth of typical raised beds and container gardens also lends perfectly to increasing the drainage in the soil. Plants need only a few things to thrive: light, nutrients, air, and water. By planting them in well-draining soil, you not only can provide them with the water they need, when they need it, but you will also remove the real possibility of drowning your plants.

That's right. Plants can and do drown. If you overwater your plants, and they are growing in heavy, clay-based soil, well the water will pool around their roots, and starve them of air. Drowning them.

I could go on, but I am sure you have the idea already. Raised bed and container gardening provides you with a host of benefits when it comes to growing your own food. While they might not turn you into Jamie Durie, they should impress your friends and family, especially those that like fresh food. And that one mate we all have that eats fast food for every meal, maybe you can teach them how good fresh food can actually be.

Grandma's Homemade Meals

Homemade food. That simple sentence conjures up all sorts of images for most people. But the most common one will be fantastic-tasting food eaten with the entire family present. And yes, that does usually include that one uncle with questionable political views, or the weird friend of your sister who always happens to be over when dinner is served. But the core memory is food. Bloody tasty food.

Now, it is your turn to step up and show your friends and family just how amazing homemade dinner can be even now that grandma is no longer around.

You've tried her recipes, but what you got was mediocre at best, not amazing. What did you do wrong?

Nothing. You just cooked with dull, boring ingredients. Unless your raw ingredients shine with goodness and flavour, you cannot expect the finished dish to also shine.

And the key to amazingly flavoured food? Raised bed and container gardening. It is as simple, and complex, as that. You will have control over what goes into your food. How your plants are cared for, and when they are harvested.

I guess the simplest way to summarize the benefits of raised bed and container gardening is as follows: With the supply chain stretching only to your backyard, you can harvest your food at peak ripeness, in the quantity you need today, and never have to worry about any contamination. You control every aspect of the plant's growth, from seed to harvest, to ensure you have the perfect produce. And to top it all off, you will never have to throw away that head of lettuce or cringe at the price of Lebanese cucumbers at Woolies ever again.

Not to mention, you will be creating those core memories with your friends and family. Happy, healthy, laughter-filled meals made with amazing fresh food you grew yourself.

Roma tomato   beefsteak tomato   cherry tomato

All Those Choices!

I bet there are days that you are a bit sick and tired of the limited choices in your local grocer. Or maybe when you go to buy some tomatoes for tonight's salad, you find the shelves empty. And what if you are looking for a golden beet for that new recipe you stumbled across on TikTok? Or perhaps a purple carrot? Or iridescent corn? Or black tomatoes for that Halloween dinner? Nope, you are pretty much out of luck on each one of those at your grocer, unless you have an amazing shop owner.

But don't give up hope. All you need is a seed catalogue.

I know they can be dangerous rabbit holes as you dream about all those amazing heirloom vegetables you can grow, but before we get there, we will need to cover many other important topics. So, hold on a moment before you get carried away. Let me tell you some tricks and hints you will need to be successful.

It Has WHAT in It?!

Microplastics, BPA, *E. coli*, mycotoxins, the list is endless. All those nasty chemicals and contaminants we don't want in our food. But how do you know what is and is not in our food? Even if the food producer follows all the rules and is super diligent in putting everything they use on their labels, you still cannot be sure that their suppliers are as upfront or even know what is in their product.

So, other than not eating, which in my view is a rather limited choice, the easiest and most reliable way you can be sure of what you are eating, is to grow your own food. For better or worse, you are in control of every single step and process, from germination to harvest to meal preparation.

That way it is entirely up to you as to what is in your food. Kinda scary and exciting at the same time, isn't it? I can hear your questions. How do I know what to do? Well, don't you worry. Together, we will go over all the important details you need to know; that is why you are here today, after all. I will guide you through the entire process, and show you when, and what, you can or should be adding to your garden, if anything at all.

What Are We Eating Today?

What's on the menu tonight? You can just stroll through your raised bed or container garden and find what is ripe.

Fresh succulent tomatoes? Plump peas? Perfectly aromatic strawberries? Depends on the day, but all of this bounty, untouched by shipping delays, packaging chemicals, and errant coughs from the public, is yours to enjoy, unless you decide to share it with your family. But that is your call.

And the Rest?

I am not going to bore you with endless pages of raised-bed benefits, but there are a few that warrant mentioning.

Gardening is exercise, and really who cannot benefit from more exercise? Even if you won't say so out loud.

You will waste less food, as you know exactly how much work went into producing it. Gone are the days of randomly chopping off the celery tops and bottoms. Scrub them clean, and if they do not end up in your salad, well they make an amazing soup.

Once you have your garden harvested, you will find yourself searching out new recipes to try out with all of your hard-grown produce. Just like your grandma and her grandma did all those years ago.

Health? Yep, we are all concerned about our health. If you weren't, you wouldn't be here reading this book. So, health. Home-grown produce is usually pesticide free, as you are present daily to look after your plants and manage any pests that you discover before it's too late. Home-grown food is also typically commercial fertilizer free. You will be adding compost to improve the soil, but are unlikely to use commercial fertilizers, and subject your food and your body to their effects.

There will be much more fruit, berries, and vegetables in your diet. I did not realize just how much of a difference it makes until I had thirty-five pounds of tomatoes sitting on the counter just waiting to be dealt with. All the snack-size ones tended to vanish. They are so incredibly tasty and easy to grab as you walk by.

I have intentionally left the most common reason why people gravitate towards raised bed or container gardening until the end. I wanted to see if I could convince you that there are many reasons to grow your food.

Money. So, the most common reason people will take up raised bed or container gardening is to save money. And yes, you will save money if you are diligent with your garden care. It is inevitable. But the trade-off is work. No longer can you just binge Netflix after dinner. However, the good thing is that you won't want to.

Your plants will need daily attention, and before you know it, you will want to give it to them. Soon, you will eagerly run to the garden to experience the joy of watching them grow, keep pests at bay, and ensure they have enough water and nutrients to live their best lives, but I digress. We will get to all this soon enough.

Chapter 2:

Not Yet! Before We Begin...

Step 1: It's All in the Preparation

I can feel your excitement even now. You just want to jump up, grab some dirt, and throw your seeds into it. The thought of all that mouth-watering food you'll grow is just buzzing through your body.

But hold on a sec. Before you get too wild and crazy, there are a few preparations that we need to cover. I am pretty sure you don't want to go to all the effort of growing your plants, only to find out you have the wrong type of soil, and the carrots taste like mud. Or the water you used contaminated your crop, making it all unfit to eat.

Patience, my friend. We will cover everything you need to know to make a successful, productive raised bed or container garden, but one step at a time.

So, take a deep breath, and relax. We are about to undertake an amazing journey. It is important that the preparations are all in place.

Common Mistakes

Let's start with the annoying, ugly side of gardening. Mistakes.

Yes, we all make mistakes. Thankfully they usually go by unnoticed by those around you, but occasionally we do make a public fool of ourselves. And when that happens, well stand up, brush yourself off, and laugh with everyone else. It happens to the best of us.

However, when it comes to raised bed and container gardening, you can do better. Learn from my mistakes. And you know what? I am going to tell you all of the embarrassing details of what I did wrong, and how you can avoid them. Pretty generous of me, isn't it?

Ready? Got your notebook and pencil? Write this in pencil so once you have understood it, you can erase any evidence of what I've said. That way only you and I will know you are not a natural-born gardener.

So, where to start?

Location

Everything is about location. How much you pay for your house, for parking your car, your grocery bill, and your view from your house. Location affects everything we do. How many of us would love that oceanside mansion or that second house in the country? Their location makes this out of reach for most people.

But the location of your raised bed or container garden brings the incredible world of succulent, fresh food not only into your reach, but into your kitchen. No longer do you need a superstar budget to eat fresh, healthy food. All you need is a portion of your yard or balcony that gets some sunshine.

If you happen to live on the side of the apartment block that gets no sunshine, or your yard is shaded all day long, don't worry. There are solutions. We will dive into light in a later chapter, but for now, the important concept is location.

So, what is an ideal, or at least adequate, location? It is a pretty short list. First, some sunlight. Second, somewhere it will be watered when it rains—that saves you some work. And last, somewhere that allows you access to all sides of the raised beds, or containers. You do need to be able to access your garden to both care for it and harvest your produce.

Water

Everything needs water. Some may not like it, such as your cat, but they need it. The same applies to your garden. Plants need water, even those funky air plants you see sometimes at the checkout at your grocers.

Edible plants need more water than flowers and other architectural plants. Why? Which do you prefer to snack on, a plump, juicy tomato or a raisin? I prefer the tomato, and a tomato plant needs a fair bit of water to ripen a perfect tomato.

So, what does that mean to me?

Is there water available at your chosen location? Is there a hose? A collection barrel for rainwater? Or do you need to carry in bucket after bucket from your sink?

Considerations. Water is heavy. And while this might be romantic initially, after the tenth bucketful first thing in the morning, it does get tiresome.

If you do have to pack in water, then I would give thought to the types of plants you want to grow, unless you can see the farmer carry of full water buckets as part of your daily workout.

We will cover in a coming chapter the many ways you can water your plants, how often is best, and how much. It would be a shame to either drown, or dry out, all those potentially amazing salads and snacks.

Bigger Is Better

Another common mistake is to make your raised bed, or container, too large. Hands up who else likes the thought of a large, productive garden? Figured it was all of us. But you do not want to put all your plants in one raised bed.

I made that mistake when I first started gardening. Three huge raised beds, waist high, over two arm spans wide and longer than I am tall. What a disaster.

Not only did it cost me more than a small fortune to fill them with dirt, but I was also unable to reach into the middle to weed or harvest my produce. But wait, there is more bad news. When it rained, I soon learned I should have gotten a builder to make them. One night of heavy rain later, and I woke to several large mud puddles on my patio.

The walls of my raised beds had collapsed, unable to contain the now heavy, wet mud. It also killed all my plants and took me a week to clean them all up. So, please learn from my mistakes.

When you build or buy, your raised beds, try to keep them no wider than your arm span, and build up on legs, not resting on the ground. This will allow you easy access to the entire growing area and give a place for the extra rainwater to drain out. You will thank me. As for length, whatever fits in your space.

Material Choice

There is a great deal of leeway when it comes to what you want to make your raised beds or containers from. Plastic, metal, old bathtubs, and even unused suitcases can be pressed into service and will make decent growing containers. If you have a stack of bricks, Besser blocks, or even a load or two of concrete, and you know how to make forms, these can also make great raised beds or containers. But there is one material you do need to stay away from. No matter how hard your mate tries to get you to take the leftovers from his fence, just say "no." What about that tempting pile of lumber in the abandoned lot down the road? Nope.

You guessed it. Pressure-treated wood.

The toxins in the lumber will leach into your soil, doing precisely what they are designed to do: killing whatever they come in contact with. So, just don't do it.

If you plan to grow organic food—and really who would not prefer that? —then the last thing you want is pressure-treated wood in your garden. If it is found anywhere on commercial growing operations, even if it is just a pole to hold the watering hose up off the ground, then that entire location cannot be classified as organic. Yes, they are that bad.

So, stay clear of pressure-treated lumber.

Plant Size

Yes, contrary to popular belief, size does matter.

You need to match your plants to your raised beds or containers. In that perfect garden you see in your head, all the plants are well-spaced, lush, and happy? Thought so.

The secret to happy plants is to give them enough space to grow. They need room. And this refers to both plants' spacing from each other and also the space they are growing in. If you have a hankering for fresh cabbage, well you are going to need a much larger growing space than if you prefer the delicate nuances of fresh homegrown celery, or plump cherry tomatoes.

Give thought to what you want to grow, as this may indicate the type and size of growing space you will need. Or vice versa, your available space may limit the types of plants you can expect to grow successfully.

Dirt, Mud, Soil

It comes in many forms and under many names. Plants need it, we hate it in our house. You might think you can just dig up some of your lawn, or your neighbors', if they are the friendly type, and put that in your raised beds or containers. Well, I don't want to say you would be wrong to do that, but you would be wrong to do that. Yard dirt—it can be a stretch to call it soil as we will discuss in a coming chapter—is suitable only as a last resort. If the only two options are not growing at all, or using dirt from your lawn, then please get digging. You will run into weed issues, unknown soil nutrient and pH levels, and possible contamination. These can all be managed, if that is your only option.

But if you can swing the price—and now remember, I am talking about those shrink-wrapped blocks of soil your garden supply house sells—to garden with, then you really ought to be rich enough to hire a gardener. They are bloody expensive and can cost more than the food you are going to grow. So, now that it is out in the open, we can forget about those shrink-wrapped bundles of expense.

The soil I am talking about is that pile of dirt off to the side at that landscape place you pass on the way to work or the weed-infested topsoil they sell at the garden supply store. Don't let the carpet of weeds discourage you, they are annual, shallow-rooted types that are growing there because it is good soil.

Once you get some of this back to your garden, we will go over what you need to do to turn this into that super-high-grade soil in the shrink-wrapped cubes. And it is less work than you think.

So, what other mistakes should I mention?

Protection

No, not that type of protection. We are talking about protection from sun, rain, frost, and pests.

"But didn't you just say that I need my raised beds in the sunshine?"

True, but not all plants need, or can handle, full sunlight. When we get into talking about what plants to grow and if you consider companion planting, then some plants can be used to shade those that prefer less light, but if you are growing a full bed of tomatoes that prefer full direct sun and they are suffering, then we will need figure out how to put up some shade cloth.

If your growing location is exposed to rain and wind, then some sort of wind barrier would also need to be considered. The last thing you want to see after a storm is all your tender, young plants broken at the base and face down in the soil.

Rain can do as much damage, especially if you live in an area that gets tropical storms. In this case, you may need to cover your raised beds or containers if you can, or make sure they have plenty of large drainage holes in the bottom. If we cannot stop the water from coming into the growing space, we need to make sure that it can escape in a timely manner. Most plants cannot manage more than a couple days with their roots submerged.

What other protection can we give your garden? How about some mulch? For being nothing more than a layer of chipped wood or straw or even ripped up newspaper, mulch can do some pretty amazing things. It can help keep water in the soil. The top layer of the mulch will dry out in the sun, creating a crust of sorts that helps keep the rest of the moisture in the soil contained for the plants to use.

Mulch can also help regulate the temperature of the soil. Plants are as fussy as we are. Too hot and they wilt and suffer. And unless you are an amazing gardener, then your plants will not be able to come inside and enjoy your air conditioning.

And weeds. We cannot forget about weeds, while some of them are scraggly and others beautiful, they will never stop trying to invade your garden. Mulch will have a huge impact on the number of weeds you have to deal with. The hot, dry surface that mulch presents to any errant seeds is very inhospitable.

If a weed, regardless of its aesthetics, does manage to get established and germinate, well the roots will only be in the top layer of mulch, and can easily be plucked out on one of your many daily visits.

The last mistake we need to look at for now, and don't worry you will discover many more as you learn to garden, is not providing enough support. Trellises, stakes, string- supports come in as many shapes and types as there are plants and people. Some plants need help standing up, while others need help holding up all their fruit, while some others manage to do the entire thing by themselves.

And Now for Some Good News

Well, we have covered the pitfalls and common mistakes, so let's shake off that depression and get into the fun part of raised-bed gardening. The plants.

Bushy, fruit-filled tomato plants, pepper plants groaning under all those ripe capsicums, sweet, tender lettuce just begging to go into your salad. We all have those dreams, or why would we be looking to grow our own plants?

And do you know what the great thing is? All that amazing fresh produce is within your grasp, not to mention the cost savings, healthier diet, and opportunity to teach your family and friends about the benefits of growing your own food.

The last time you wandered through the plant nursery—or DIY store depending on where you live and who sells seeds and plants—you will have run into rack after rack after rack of pre-packaged seeds, and then in the live plant section, well, thousands of young plants.

So, where do you start?

Well, raised-bed gardening is like so many things in life. The better the preparation, the better the results. Take a moment and reflect. Why do you want to grow plants in a raised bed? What is drawing you here? While I cannot speak directly for you, I can hazard a few guesses that I think will be pretty close to the mark.

Why Am I Here?

Firstly, the current cost of food has prompted you to look into alternatives to feed yourself, and your friends and family if you are a kind-hearted type, and of course you are, like all other gardeners.

I expect you are not alone in your shock about current produce prices. A head of lettuce for $11.99. Unbelievable. While there has been a 12.7% hike in the consumer price index, this is only part of the picture. Floods in Queensland and NSW have damaged the Lockyer Valley, cooler temperatures have delayed harvests, a 120% increase in fertilizer costs, and to top it all off, unstable world politics have combined to drive prices mad (Kelly, 2022).

Secondly, you have a curiosity about growing your own food. Can you do it? Of course you can! This is what I am going to teach you all about. By the time we part company, you will have a flourishing garden of your own, and will start thinking about hassling your friends into starting their own. And trust me, you will have the skills and know how to teach them. It's true.

And thirdly, you have always loved a garden. Your parents, or grandparents had one and you have fond childhood memories of time amongst the plants. Together, we will journey down the memory, and before you know it, you will have your own garden to inspire your children, nieces and nephews, or even the neighborhood kids.

Now that we have figured out why you are here, we need to think about plants, and what you are looking to get from them.

One of the main considerations, as this has a direct effect on what you plant, is what is your goal? A beautiful, flower-filled space with some edible plants scattered about, or a veritable forest of food at your fingertips?

I am going to work with the forest of food idea, as you can just tone it down and add flowers for a great looking space.

That Looks Good Enough to Eat

Food. What do you like to eat? If you don't like broccoli, then don't plant it. If you absolutely cannot get enough fresh tomatoes in your life, then focus on them.

What I am getting at is one of the big mistakes both new and experienced gardeners make is to plant edible crops that they do not like to eat. In my mind, that is a waste of time and energy, unless they provide some other benefit to you than sustenance.

Now, this is the fun part about plants: Varieties. When was the last time you ate a purple potato, or a white carrot, or a black tomato? I don't know either, but you can grow them.

Spend an evening on the net looking into seeds. It is a very, very slippery rabbit hole, so do not be surprised if you lose the entire evening. But when you resurface, come back and we can discuss yields, planting density, and care.

How was your trip? I can imagine you found supply houses that will sell you hundreds of varieties of tomatoes and let's not mention the squashes, the potatoes, carrots, and beets. A tad overwhelming, isn't it?

I wanted to plant them all when I first discovered those seed catalogs, but I am going to suggest you leave seeds for next year. And yes, there will be a next year, and a next. Gardening is that addictive.

What I am going to suggest is you head to your local garden supply house and look at their live plants. Keep in mind what you actually want to eat and how many people you are looking to feed.

Typically, one plant of each type that interests you per person for the first year. No, this will not fill your freezer with food, but it will give you good variety, and a decent amount of produce so you can decide what you want to grow next year.

But back to my point. The garden supply store will have thousands of little plants, all waiting for you to take them home. Look for the most numerous varieties of each type of plant you want to grow. Odds are these are what everyone else is growing, and this variety will grow well at your location.

Now that you have your tray or box of seedlings back home, you need to keep them damp, and get them into the soil as soon as possible. Greenhouses and garden stores will usually water their plants at least twice a day to keep them looking good for the customer. If you can get your seedlings into the soil the same day, then you will lessen the transplant shock, and keep your plant looking good.

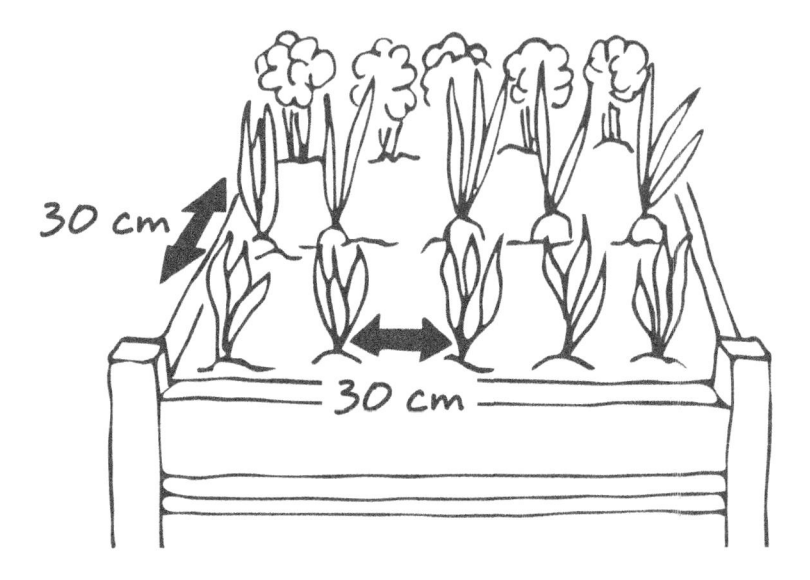

Not So Close

The next step is a hard one. And I know you are going to struggle with this for the rest of your life. Spacing. Yep, plant spacing. It is a skill I have yet to come to grips with after all these years.

Plants need space. For example, take that small butter lettuce in your hand. I bet you figure you could plant one every ten centimetres apart. Lots of room to grow, and it will look good. All the soil used. Job done.

Nope. Lettuce needs 30 to 45 centimetres between plants on average. Yeah, that much. Now, once you put your seeds or seedlings in, your raised bed will be full of empty soil and a couple plants. But when your plants are ready to harvest, if you planted them at 45 centimetre pacing, then the leaves will not quite touch, and they will be tender and full.

On the other hand, if you plant your seeds and seedlings like I do and cram them all together, when you go to harvest them in a couple months, the leaves will be all packed, stunted, and unappealing. So please, do better than me and pay attention to the plant spacing. It will provide you with much better results in the end.

It Is All About... Timing

Isn't this the truth? Timing. If you had only made your move sooner, that hottie would be sharing your kitchen with you, or asked for that promotion or found the courage to adopt that perfect pet you had dreamed about since childhood.

Timing can change your life. And the same can be said for your garden. Get the timing right, and your plants will thrive. Get it wrong, and they will drown or freeze or just be grumpy and unhappy.

This is where you would expect a timing chart for the most common garden plants isn't it? Yeah, thought so. But you see, the problem here is size. If you live in the north, then your timing will be radically different to someone living in the south.

Head down to your garden supply store—don't worry, you will remember their names soon enough and become fast friends—and ask them for the best planting dates for your local area. They are the local experts on this and many more things you will come to learn.

A quick summary is in order here. Start your garden with live seedlings, they are inexpensive and will, if cared for well, provide you with many times their purchase cost on fresh produce over the growing season. Grow the foods you like to eat. That sounds simple, but trust me, you will be dragged off the path by some exotic-looking plant that may turn out to be not to your taste, so leave that until next year.

Plant your seeds at the correct spacing, that information is also provided by those incredibly knowledgeable and friendly folks at your local garden supply store. And finally, plant your plants at the right time.

Sounds pretty simple. And it is! Some of the most common plants to start a raised-bed garden are beans, lettuce, tomatoes, cucumbers, and herbs. Try these first. They are simple to look after, and let you get your fingers into the dirt with some tasty rewards for your work.

Wow, That Is Bright!

Sunshine. Some people love it, some try to avoid it. Your plants are the same. Some, like tomatoes, love a full sunny day, while others, like lettuce, would rather hide under that beach umbrella.

Light plays an important part in the success of your raised-bed garden. Knowing which plants to plant where, and how much light they get, can have a significant impact on your harvest yields.

So how do you know which plant likes what? There are a couple simple ways to learn. Ask your new friends at the garden store, or head over to your local DIY, or wherever seeds are sold, and take a picture with your phone of the seed packages of the plants you bought.

Each seed pack will have a few cryptic lines and graphics that are intended to tell you everything you need to know about the seeds inside. You will see spacing, seed depth, and other words like full sun or partial shade or some little graphics with sun and shade type things in it.

Snap a pic. It will help you remember it.

But what does it mean? Full sun, partial shade, full shade, shade tolerant, sun tolerant. The variations are endless, but they come down to a few general categories.

Category	Definition
Full Sun/Full Exposure	Unobstructed sunshine for six to eight hours a day. The plant may still grow in less-than-ideal sun coverage but will not produce as much as it could. These plants typically will not survive indoors without supplemental lighting.
Partial Sun/Partial Shade	The plant can handle a few hours a day of full sun without harm, and likewise a few hours a day of shade will not stunt the growth. These plants will survive and grow well indoors in a bright sun filled window.
Full Shade	The plant requires a shaded or indirect light to grow, but still needs to be in bright light. These plants will survive indoors but will not thrive.

Now, I don't expect you will have your raised beds indoors, but the indoor equivalents provide a frame of reference that we can all understand. But what about that side yard, or backyard that does not get much or any direct sunlight? You can of course still grow plants, but the variety and type of plant may be more limited than if you had sunshine. So, what does this mean in practical terms?

If you can, look at your potential space several times during the day and map out where the most light is. This is where you would ideally place your raised-bed or container garden. Remember that even reflected light is better than none.

With the location determined, then you will need to look at the light requirements for the plants you would like to grow. Given a lack of direct sunlight, you will be limited to shade-tolerant and shade-requiring plants. This is not to say that sun-loving plants like tomatoes will not grow for you. They will, but they will grow slowly and likely will have less and smaller fruit.

A raised-bed garden without direct sunlight can still grow abundant salad greens, beets, *Brassicas*, carrots, garlic, and potatoes. You will need to buy your tomatoes, but even a side yard with no direct sun can provide most of your salad and fresh vegetable needs.

And let's not forget about herbs. Many herbs will grow quite happily in low light areas. They will grow slower than if in direct sunlight, but they will still grow. Oregano, thyme, coriander, mint, rosemary, parsley, and basil will grow almost as well in the shade as in the sun. So, keep this in mind if you have a full raised-bed garden, but still want to grow some herbs, or if you want to add some vegetables to your garden and have run out of room from all the herbs you planted.

Depending on your location, is there the possibility of a few containers placed in an area that does get some sunlight? Down the side of the driveway? At the front of the building? A single 20-litre bucket, with good soil and sunlight can produce all the tomatoes you would need for summer eating.

If you have space for two or three buckets, then abundant capsicums and cucumbers can be yours as well.

So, we have light figured out, well at least enough for growing our plants. Now we need to talk about putting your plants in soil.

Get Them in the Dirt

If you are one of those fortunate people with a bright, sunny growing space, well, go get a drink and come back once we have caught up. The rest of us need to talk about shade.

Shade can be nice on a hot day for sure. But not so good on a cold day. And not surprisingly your plants feel the same. They prefer sunshine on a cold day and shade on a hot one. The amount of shade you must contend with can be a deciding factor in the size of your raised beds or if you need to go to more individual containers to grow your plants.

Everything comes down to the space you have to grow in. And unless you are kind enough to invite me over for tea—and I take it with sugar and no milk—I will have to do my best to cover the big picture concerns you will face and leave it up to you to sort out the details.

Large patches of sun, slowly ambling across your backyard are ideal for a few good-sized raised beds. Lots of space for plants, lots of sunlight. Ideal.

While a sun-dappled space does look romantic and inviting, it is less so to your plants. In this case, a large, raised bed or two might not capture enough sunlight to keep all your charges happy. If this looks to be true, then all you need to do is switch to containers.

Nothing else changes, the soil, the water, nothing. You are just dividing up your raised bed into manageable portion sizes. Now you can plant one tomato per container and place them in the sunniest patches. Your lettuce pots can either be smaller or hold several plants.

However you set up your growing space, a few raised-beds, containers, or a mix of both, you are only a few steps away from your own amazing garden. Growing in containers does change some of the plant options, due to the restricted size and depth of most common containers. Typically, you would choose from beets, chili peppers, lettuce, onions, radishes, spinach, and tomatoes. But while you must admit that this might be a limited selection of plants, they do come together to make a wonderful salad.

Write It All Down

We have covered a great deal of problems and issues, but I have left the fun part to last. Planning. No, it isn't boring, it is exciting.

You get to dream. Now is the time to figure out what you want to grow, how you want to grow it, and where you will put it. I am talking about sitting down with some paper, or your favourite tablet, making lists, drawing sketches, and fantasizing.

Now that you can see your dream garden, we need to come back to reality for a bit.

Write it all down. The big picture, the dream set up. You need a goal to make sure each small step you take in the next couple of years will be headed in the right direction. So, write it down. Good.

Now make a list of the plants you want to grow or eat. Write that down as well. I know you spotted the difference between your list of plants and mine I shared earlier. Don't worry. You will get to grow all your amazing choices, but not this year. I want you to succeed. So, I am stacking the deck, so to speak.

Now you need to get into the details. If that is not your thing, go get your friend, the one who keeps all their credit card receipts and actually checks them against their bill. You know who I am talking about. They will record the details we are looking for.

Bribe them with dinner, drinks, or whatever you need, and create the following documents. Oh, and you will need to do this each year so you can mark your progress. Right, you will need a planting layout, seeding dates, and suggested harvest dates taken off the pictures of the seed packs you took earlier.

Now you have a baseline. Come harvest you should revisit this paperwork and see how you did. Were the harvest dates close? What about yields? Did the plants survive? I know this sounds dull, boring, and pedantic but if you can do this only for a few years, you will have a really good idea of what grows well in your location and if your style of care suits your plants.

Oh, and don't forget what type of supports you made for the plants that need them. If they are adequate, overkill, or pathetic. All of this will make next year's garden much better.

We have covered common mistakes with the raised beds—well not really mistakes, more like a few things you need to keep in mind when you select your plants. This leads us into the next chapter of actually creating the raised-bed garden.

If you need a bathroom break, a coffee refill, or to split up that fight between your kids, go take care of business. But hurry back. I can guarantee you don't want to be left behind. There is some great information coming up, and it would be a shame if your neighbour got all the juicy tips instead of you.

Chapter 3:

Can You Build It? Yes, You Can

Step 2: Build Your Own Raised Bed (Or Buy It)

Welcome back. Now that you've refilled your drink, and quelled the rebellion, we can get back to raised-bed gardening.

Please hold your questions for a few minutes, if you can. Yes, you can build a raised-bed garden, even if that picture you put up last week has already fallen down. Ha, I wasn't going to mention your crooked, dodgy-looking shelves, but now that you bring them up, even if you have no skills, or are still learning when it comes to home DIY, you can still build your own raised-bed garden.

The process is the same regardless of the shape and size of your raised bed, so I am going to base our talk around a two-foot by two-foot square bed. Have a sip of your coffee and get ready.

Tools

Tools. You may have none or be the envy of Scott Cam. It doesn't matter, you can still make your own raised bed.

If you have a back shed filled with the catalogue perfect tool collection, then I will leave you to your own devices. There are things I could teach you, but they are out of the scope of this book. So off you go but come back once you have built your raised bed. We still have lots of information to cover.

Right. For those still here let's have a chat about the tools you'll need, and I would bet you have most of them already. Before we talk about specifics, we need to figure out what type of raised bed you want to build or buy.

Wood

The simplest, and thus most common raised bed is nothing more than a simple wooden frame. Before you head off to the local DIY, we need to figure out how large you want, or need, your bed to be.

How much room do you have? How long are your arms? Yeah, your arm length does come into play with gardening, after all, how are you going to reach your plants and harvest all your produce?

Keeping these two conditions in mind, you now have the size of your raised bed. If this comes out to some weird dimension, like one point three metres by two point four, then it will work better if you adjust it to the nearest quarter metre. So, your bed would come out as one point two five metres by two point five metres.

Why?

It has to do with planting your seeds, working with companion plants, and maximum yield from your plants.

Now that you have your size determined, and I am sure the number of beds as this is an exciting moment, you can head off to the lumber store, or raid your brother-in-law's shed. Your call.

But before you head off, did you know there are other options that might work better? Yeah, it's true.

Alternative Materials

All it takes is a slightly sideways view, and you will be astonished at what can be repurposed into a raised bed.

Those plastic crates filling your storage room, filled with the kid's old toys, and the like. Sell the toys, or give them away, and you have a raised bed. Might be a bit small, and will need drainage holes in the bottom, but it is a good place to start.

Oh, and those shelves you put up but are scared to put anything on? The boards will make ideal edges for a raised bed. All you need to do is join them together. The quickest way, and surprisingly accurate and strong, is to go purchase a couple of sets of door hinges. With one hinge per corner, not only will the raised bed be simple to build, but you can also pull the pins and put it all away once the growing season is over.

What else would make a good raised bed? Anyone?

Right, old bathtubs will work great, if you don't mind the slight bogan vibe. Anyone else? Kiddie pools, yep, you'll just need to put in some drain holes, and be super careful with your tools as you care for and harvest your produce. Any other ideas? What about some logs laid out in a square or rectangle? That works well. Yep, bricks, Besser blocks, even old takeaway containers, if you have enough, that is. Old shoes? Never thought about using that, but I guess if you have enough to outline your growing space, they'd work as well.

I feel you are getting the idea. Pretty much anything that can hold in your dirt will work. Now, most of these would be on the ground, and that is fine for those with young, supple backs, but those of you a bit older, and wiser—no I'm not going to ask your ages—you know as well as I that working on your knees can get a bit tiresome.

So, consider if it is possible to put a base under your raised bed so that it is up at a comfortable height. That chair with the broken back, that old table your uncle broke at the family reunion, even a couple of step ladders with a plank between them.

The more comfortable you are working in your garden beds, the more inclined you will be to work. It may not seem like a big deal to start with but working in your garden is supposed to be rewarding and fun, not a reason to see your chiropractor.

Pre-Built

Of course, there is always the option to head to your local garden supply store, or Amazon, and buy a raised bed. They come in a bewildering array of sizes, materials, and assembly styles.

One of the advantages of purchasing a raised bed is the availability of easy-fit hardware. A quick search will show you a variety of connectors designed for dimensioned lumber. All you need to do is to screw these to each end of the lumber you had cut to the correct size, and instantly, you have a raised bed.

Some hardware will also allow you to stack layers together so you can make the raised bed as tall as you would like or can afford once you go to fill it with soil.

With all these possibilities before you, pick one, or as many as you can fit, that appeal to your sense of style, into your garden space. You will be living with them for years to come, and ideally, they would also make you smile every day.

If you are headed down the smaller container route, then you will have an enormous selection of possibilities. Get creative. If it can hold soil, and either has a drain or you can put one in, then by all means use it.

That floral gumboot? Perfect for a head of lettuce or a beet plant. That iridescent plastic punch bowl? Ideal for a capsicum plant or two. Those heavy fabric shopping bags they make you use now? Filled with dirt, they make a perfect home for your cucumbers. You get the idea. Have fun with it, and let your imagination run wild. No matter what your budget is, you can create a raised-bed garden and enjoy your own fresh produce.

Now that you have your beds figured out for both size and materials, we need to talk about seeds and planting.

Chapter 4:

Let's Talk About Soil

Step 3: The Soil Mix Master

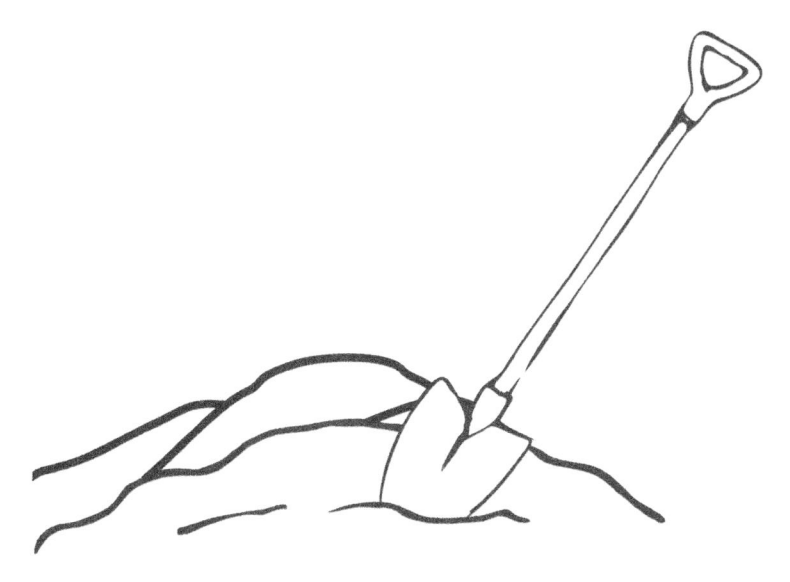

Soil. You gotta have it, your plants need it, and you will come to love it. Maybe not as much as your kids or your spouse, but you will have great affection for it. While you will still love those important people in your life, they will just need to get used to the fact you are also head over heels in love with your dirt.

Dirt, or soil when we are talking about gardening, is amazing. Besides unerringly finding that white shirt you only ever wear to the office, it nourishes, waters, and supports your plants. It's impressive that it can do any of these by itself, let alone all three at once.

Water. Put your plant in a bucket of water. Sorted. But your plant will flop over like a dead fish and drown.

Support. Drive a stake into the ground and tie your plant to it. Supported. Yes, but your plant will shrivel up and die, leaving behind a well-supported carcass.

Nourishment. Also very simple. Go buy a box of fertilizer and stuff your plant into it. Done. For sure, but the fertilizer will burn your plant like battery acid, leaving behind the shrivelled remains of your poor plant.

And yet somehow soil manages to do all this for you and doesn't even need you to text it in the morning. What it does require, however, is an ongoing commitment to improving it, but we will cover composting and other additives in a bit.

Where to Find Soil

Dirt is everywhere. Everyone knows that. It is in your yard, in your car, and even sometimes in your shoe. But finding the dirt your plants need can take a bit more effort, or money if you can afford it.

For those of you with deep pockets, off you go to the garden store. They will gladly take your money in return for a few blocks of plastic-wrapped dirt. Show us what they stuffed into the back of your car when you get back.

The rest of us will take the less expensive, and I think, much more interesting route to find soil for our garden. We have already discussed the problems with using your yard as a source for soil, and few of us can afford those pricey shrink-wrapped bales. So, what options does that leave?

Topsoil.

I expect you didn't notice that pile of dirt at the garden store. It may be out back, or just so covered in weeds that it blended in with everything else. Well, that is what we are looking for.

Most reputable garden stores will either make their own or buy it from another supplier. It will have been sifted to remove the larger chunks of clay and debris but will not have the texture you would find in the shrink-wrapped soil.

If by some chance your local garden store does not have a pile of topsoil, then head out to your local landscaping company. They will have topsoil, as that is what they do.

Buying bulk topsoil may seem like a hassle, but this is to your advantage. The shrink-wrapped soil is usually designed as potting soil, full of added nutrients and volume boosters to provide a near-perfect environment to help seedlings of all types grow.

Sounds pretty good to me. But here is the catch. Seedlings of *all types*. There are only a few things that seedlings need to grow: air, water, light, and nutrients. But like people, every seedling is different.

Some like really dense, wet soil, like cranberries or celery, while other plants prefer light drier soil, like tomatoes and peas. Given these variations, and if you are keen to garden, then you can create the perfect environment for each of your plants.

What would be better than crafting each raised bed into the perfect environment for the plants you put there? Your plants will be happier and healthier. And this can only lead to better produce, and large harvests.

So, What Makes Good Soil?

Now we get into the nitty-gritty of what is good soil and how we make it. Once you get your topsoil home, either in bags or in the back of a Ute—if you or a friend has one—there are a few things you should do before you put your plants in it.

Building Your Soil

The perfect growing soil has a ratio of 50% topsoil, 30% good compost, and 20% organic matter (Lamp'l, 2018).

Topsoil

Let's make sense of these numbers. Half of your dirt should be topsoil. That is fairly self-explanatory, as you have topsoil from the garden store or your local landscaping company. But how to make sure it is good topsoil?

Grab a handful of topsoil and squeeze it tight. What did you get? A handful of sandy soil that crumbles away when you open your hand? Or a dirt snowball, compact and imprinted with your finger impressions? Both of these are exactly what you do not want.

If the soil is too sandy, it will not hold enough water to sustain your edible plants. If it is a solid clay-like ball, then the opposite is true. Not only will the soil hold too much moisture, and potentially rot your plant's roots, it risks being too hard for good root penetration.

So, what do you want?

A perfect handful of soil is loose, moist, and crumbles like that perfect cake you spotted at the baker's last week. It should be on the dark side of brown or grey and smell nice. There should be no rancid overtones or sticky residue.

If you can find this, then your plants will love you, especially once you add your compost and organic matter. It is worth taking your time to find the best topsoil you can. Not only will this save you work in modifying your soil, but it allows your plants to produce more food, which in turn saves you more money.

If you can only find topsoil in bags at your garden store or Bunnings, then test it the same. Just don't rip open any random bag, there will almost always be one that is already split. Have a squeeze and see what you find.

Compost

I am confident you have heard the term. But just what is it? In the simplest of terms, compost is rotted vegetable matter. Nothing more, nothing less.

By piling all your leftover vegetable waste like peelings and cut-off bits and dinner plate scraps, they will decompose into a wonderful soil additive. Compost is an amazing product. Filled with nutrients from the food you have already paid for and is ideally suited for your plants to use.

We all have that friend with the bucket of rotten fruit under their counter. Yep, that's compost. But you don't have to have that smelly thing in your kitchen if you don't want to. Go have a quick look through Amazon when you go get your drink refilled, and you will see hundreds of kitchen compost bins, with sealing lids and odour filters.

The other option, which is the one I prefer, is to have a large compost bin outside in your yard. And after each meal, simply take your scraps out and add them to the growing pile. Instead of paying for fertilizer for your plants, you can save all that money by simply letting nature transform your scraps into fertilizer.

So, I hear your question. "What can I compost?"

If you are a vegetarian, then I would guess all of your scraps will be vegetable based and ideal for composting. For carnivores, there are a few helpful guidelines to follow. Don't put any plastic, metal, wood, etc. in your compost. That makes sense, but you also need to exclude any meat scraps—as they will attract vermin—and anything oily. The oil will go rancid and attract flies and other undesirable creatures.

The good news is you can compost eggshells, tea bags, and coffee grounds, but check with the manufacturers about the coffee filters.

There are dozens of things you can add to your compost that will add nutrients and volume to your soil, but some of the best are in the table here.

Material	Benefits
Leaves	Aged leaves are an ideal addition to add bulk and nutrients to your soil. If you do not have any, I can almost be certain one of your neighbours will be glad to let you take theirs. Ask around, and be that good neighbour.
Mineral Soil	Along with nutrients, plants need minerals, just like us. Typically, this is from the bedrock beneath the soil, but if

	that is not enough, then mineral soil will add a great boost of minerals directly to your compost and then your soil.
Vermicompost (Worm Castings)	Worm poop. Expensive, but very high in nitrogen, which promotes leaf growth, phosphorus, which promotes soil nutrient uptake, and potassium, which promotes root growth and efficient water uptake
Mushroom Compost	The leftover growing media from commercial mushroom cultivation is high in nitrogen, potassium, magnesium, and calcium. This may be an inexpensive alternative to worm poop.
Bark Chips	Usually available from landscaping companies, these chips will add bulk to your soil as the material decomposes.
Cow or Poultry Manure	Once well-composted—this may take a year or two—these manures will provide excellent nutrients to your soil. These can be purchased in prepacked bags, ready to add to your soil, but I would recommend even these are composted for a year. This should kill off any unknown pests and most of the persistent herbicides that may have been in the animal feed.

That all seems pretty good, doesn't it? Yeah, but there are a few things you should consider carefully before you add them to your compost bin. Have a glance at this table before you get carried away by adding extras to your garden.

Material	Problem
Horse Manure	Persistent herbicides. Unless you know, with certainty, that the horses producing the manure were not fed grasses and such that were treated with persistent herbicides, such as Clopyralid, Aminopyralid, or Picloram, then do not tempt your luck. Any persistent herbicide like these, or others, will survive the horse, and the composting heat, and then kill off your plants. So, it is best to be safe and avoid horse manure.
Peat Moss	Once a staple in gardening, used for bulking up your soil, and improving water retention, it is no longer recommended. Needing hundreds of years to create, peat moss is not a sustainable option, and there are many better options on the market.
Artificial Fillers	Those crushed milk containers, or soft-drink cans in the bottom of your pots to fill up some space and add drainage. There is no need. If you want to fill the bed to try and save on soil costs, then the best approach is hügelkultur. This just means adding branches and small logs under your soil. These will slowly break down and add nutrients to your soil while they fill the bottom third of your bed, saving you money on expensive soil.
Fill Dirt	Any dirt that is not soil. The leftover excavation dirt from the new house down the block, the dirt under your grass. As tempting as it may be to use other dirt, and not soil, to fill your raised beds, these will defeat all effort, time, and money you are putting into your soil to make it

	perfect. If you need a filler, then use branches and the like as we said above.
Biochar	You may run across this at your garden store and wonder if you should use it. If you have thick, heavy soil, which is unlikely given the testing you did of your soil before you bought it, then adding the biochar will provide aeration and assist in moisture absorption.
Fire Ash	A limited amount of wood fire ash will help change the pH of your soil, you can get testing kits at your local garden store, but you should never add any charcoal ash to your soil. Charcoal briquettes contain chemical additives that will harm your plants.
Mycorrhizae	A beneficial fungus that may or may not help your plants. With no way to test if the fungus in the bag is compatible, or even symbiotic, with the existing fungus in your topsoil, it could be a waste of money and time to add it.

Organic Matter

And finally, the 20% organic matter. So, what is organic matter? Pretty much anything natural. Grass clippings, leaves, branches, and seaweed if you live near the coast. The organic matter will keep the soil from compacting too much, keeping good air penetration into the soil and reducing root growth problems. Organic matter will also work in tandem with your compost to keep moisture in the soil and available to the roots of your plants.

Once you have harvested your crops, which we will cover in an upcoming step, you can add all the stalks, leaves, and inedible plant parts to your compost pile. They will decompose, and your plants next year will benefit from this year's nutrients. A great nutrient circle.

Making Your Very Own Compost Bin

This can be nothing more than a cardboard box against the far fence all the way up to automated rotating bins powered by self-contained solar panels.

And yeah, who doesn't like the idea of robots doing your work? But seriously, compost bins are even easier to make than raised beds. All you need is something to hold your vegetable scraps, lawn clippings, and leaves. If you are careful to exclude non-vegetable food waste, then it is likely you will not even have to cover it.

But most compost bins should have a mesh cover of some sort to keep out the local wildlife. Try and make sure the lid is not solid. You want the rain to water your compost. Otherwise, you will be responsible for it, and I am sure you have your hands full with your new garden.

Take all the thought you put into your raised beds and simplify it. Good compost bins will give you easy access to each side, as you should mix up the contents a couple times a year to promote even decomposition. They also keep the soil in one place, and yet are situated in such a manner as to allow easy unloading into your wheelbarrow or bucket.

The observant among you—alright all of you—noticed that I have not said your compost bins should be this size or made from this or that material. Those decisions are up to you. You know your yard space, the availability of scrap wood, old shipping pallets, or disused recycling bins far better than I. The only advice I will pass along is to try and size your bins for about three to four months' waste.

In an ideal setup you would have four to eight smaller compost bins that you rotate through. By the time you get back to the first one, usually after a year or more, you will have a bin full of beautiful black gold. Yeah, that is the perfect world scenario. Reality usually looks much different.

A single larger compost bin will work as well. You will need to mix it up more often and may fill it up before all the material has composted, but this will still provide a compost supply for your garden. Start small and grow as you need. If you find you have filled your first bin, and it has not transformed into compost yet, start another bin if you have the space.

The more compost you can provide to your plants, the more free fertilizer they get, and the bigger and better the produce will be. Remember, compost is all about transforming the nutrients in the food you have already paid for and letting it be used to grow the food you will eat after harvest.

Seedlings Are Sensitive

Like all children, seedlings are a fussy bunch. Think about baby food. Nutritious, easy to swallow, and kinda bland. Well, that also described the ideal soil for seedlings. Not too many nutrients, or they may burn the new, delicate roots. The soil should hold enough moisture for these new roots, but not so much as to be waterlogged. And we cannot forget about air. This ideal soil must also have enough texture to ensure there is adequate air supply to the roots without drying them out.

Sounds like a delicate balancing act to me. So, how do we do it?

We start with some compost. If this is your first year gardening and you do not yet have your compost system up and running, do not worry. Go grab a bag or two of readymade compost from your garden store. This should be light and fluffy, so take your time to make sure you have the best bag you can find.

Before you head home, also pick up a bag, or block, of coconut coir. This is nothing more than the husk of the coconut, all those fibres and such, cleaned and bagged. Coconut coir is a great product to add to any heavy, dense soil as it adds volume and water absorption to your raised beds or containers. It is going to serve the same purpose for your seedlings.

Don't forget to grab a bag of perlite. That white, Styrofoam-type stuff you sometimes find in dried flower arrangements. Look for a bag about half the size of your compost. We don't need as much to make the seedling soil, and there is no point wasting your money and buying more than you need.

Now that you have your coconut coir, your compost, and your perlite, all you have to do is mix it all together. Well, almost. If your coconut comes in a bag, you are ready to go. However, some coconut comes in a compressed block. If this is what you've found, then you need to rehydrate this before moving on.

Open it up and put it in a big shopping bag, your bathtub, or even a rubbish bin with a clean liner. Add water and wait. You will be surprised just how much water it will take. Keep adding water and breaking apart the wet material. The end goal is to have your container, or bag, filled with damp coconut that has no lumps in it.

Those of you with the bags of coconut can put down your drinks and join us again. Get an empty shopping bag, or bucket, and fill it just under half with the compost. Add the coconut coir and mix well. When you are happy, then add the perlite. Ideally, you should put in about half as much perlite as the compost and coconut coir. Now you get to mix some more. The coconut will stick to your fingers, the compost will get under your nails, and the perlite will be stubborn and not mix in very well. But keep at it.

This will take longer than you think, but once it is all mixed, you can wipe off your hands and cover the bucket. This seedling mixture needs to stay moist, or your baby plants will shrivel up and die. Put this aside until we get to the chapter on seeding, and then we will show you how to use it.

Mulch

What is it? In the simplest form, it is something that covers the soil in your raised beds. That's all. But of course, like everything else, there is much more to mulch than that. Mulch can be used to change the aesthetics of your garden, add water absorption capability to your soil, help control weeds, and delineate areas where you can walk, and should not.

With the broad uses of mulch, it can be divided into two general categories, organic and inorganic.

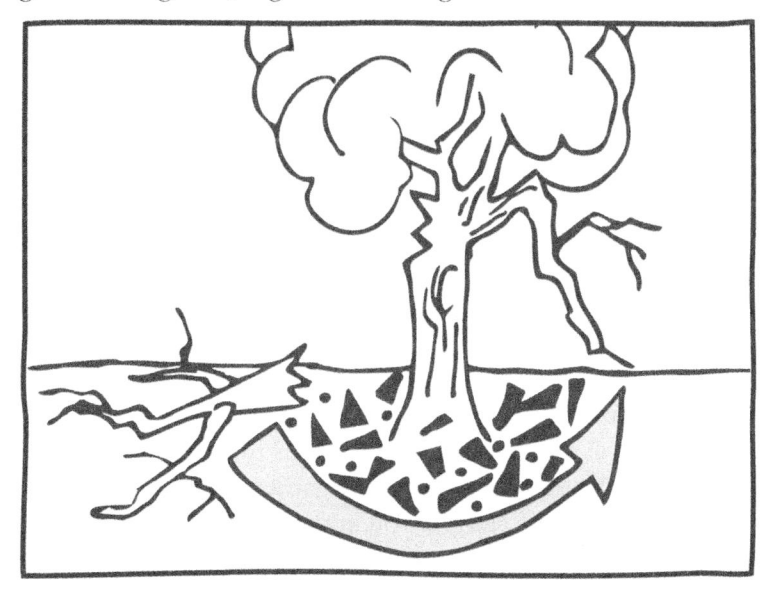

Organic

Organic mulches are what you will see in your local parks. It is all that chipped wood and bark that covers the ground underneath all the plants. Depending on your local government, they may also use tree mulch on the trails, but this is becoming less and less common as it does require more work to replace as people wear it away as they walk. Organic mulches also tend to be more slippery when wet, thus providing some health and safety problems, and encouraging the use of inorganic mulches like gravel and recycled tires.

Organic mulch is typically made from all the trees and shrubs that were pruned throughout the city over the last season. There is little thought given to the impact this mix of organic matter might have on the soil, other than aesthetics, moisture trapping, and weed control. Now here is an opportunity to learn from these gardeners. They are paid to look after these public spaces, and the less work they have to do the easier their job is.

So, what does this mean to you, the backyard raised-bed gardener? Well, if you grab a handful of mulch next time you are in the park, take a close look at it. You'll likely see chunks of trees, bushes, leaves, and other random organic material in all shapes and sizes. This type of mulch will decompose into the soil at different rates, providing a slow release of nutrients as it does. While you can use sifted mulch, and it will work quite well and look very sharp in the process, it is usually cheaper to get general-purpose mulch.

Depending on your location, there may be some trees that should not be used as mulch cover as they may change the pH of the soil or release other chemicals that could harm your plants. So, head down to your garden supply store, and have a chat with the staff. If you know them well enough, then make sure you bring a six-pack or bottle of their favourite wine to butter them up.

The staff will know all the local flora, which can be used as mulch, and which species cannot. Such an untapped resource, and all for the price of a few drinks.

Another option is to wander through the garden store and see what they have for bulk, or ready-bagged mulches. They are likely to have a few choices but keep in mind they will tend to be expensive.

The option I like to try, and if it fails then I head to the garden store, is to contact your local arborist. They usually have a huge pile of chipped trees that they have to pay to get rid of. A few kind words and they may let you have all you can carry. Another option, which depends again on your local government, is their gardening staff. Some locations have programs to assist urban gardeners, providing soil, and mulches, and some even give away seeds. Worth a few phone calls and visits, I think.

Now, if you have family, or friends that live in the country, or have anything to do with animals, then they may have silage or hay laying around. This is a brilliant mulch as it lets the water flow past, keeping the soil hydrated, but the surface will dry out and keep out weed seeds. Straw or hay can also be worked into the soil or buried with next year's compost if you practice no-till gardening, whereas the tree mulch should be removed as much as possible to keep the texture of the soil fine and crumbly.

Inorganic

So, what do I mean by inorganic mulches? This is also a broad category that covers everything from chipped-up recycled tires used in kids' playgrounds, to random pieces of metal and tarps, to gravel and stone.

With the definition of mulch so broad, pretty much anything you use to cover your garden can be seen as mulch. But practically, mulch is usually only a few different items.

A common landscaping cover is gravel, and this can range from pea gravel all the way up to small boulders. Gravel provides great pest protection, pretty good weed protection, and some water retention. But as you can plainly see, it is not really ideal for your raised bed, other than the pathways around your yard.

Ground-up recycled tires are another common mulch. With a never-ending supply of the raw material, and the increasing availability of the chips, this gives good weed protection and water retention. Being soft and comfortable to walk on, it makes great path coverings but does little for pest control. This is commonly used in locations where people and children might enter the garden space.

Organic tree mulch is occasionally placed under a wire mesh, like chicken wire or a fine builder's mesh. While not pleasant to walk on, this combination will provide good water retention, good weed control, and good pest control. Most insects will struggle to get through the tree mulch, while cats, dogs, and other larger pests will shy away from the metal mesh.

Of the three broad types of inorganic mulch, only the combination of tree bark and mesh coil is suitable for your raised beds. If you find, like I do, that your neighbourhood tomcat continues to dig up your garden, then a layer of chicken wire will drive him away.

You need to be careful putting the chicken wire in place, both regarding your hands, and your plants. By the second year of growing, you will know if there are problem animals around, and if so, you can place the chicken wire as you transplant your seedlings into the bed. Just be sure to leave adequate space around the plant stalks to keep them clear of the chicken wire.

End of the Season

We need to jump forward in time for a few minutes. Don't worry, it is a quick trip.

Here we are, seven months in the future. You didn't even feel the transition, did you? Good. So, why are we here? To discuss what happens to all your compost, potting soil, and raised bed soil once you have harvested your crops and are preparing for winter. Wait, are any of you from the tropics? You, you, and you. Well, off you go back to today. You can grow all year round, so don't need to worry about this.

Right, now that they are gone, we can get back to business. Post-harvest cleanup. We will start with all the plant stalks and inedible portions. Cut them into small enough pieces to fit into your compost bin or bins. You want to make sure you only put healthy, dead plants in there. If any of your pants have had powdery mildew or any fungus growths, then keep those dead plants aside. They will contaminate your compost and spread their problems into next year's garden. Chuck them in the garbage or burn them if you are allowed to have fires.

If you have any fallen leaves or lawn clippings handy, then cover the healthy, dead plants in your compost bins. They will do their work and should be transformed into good soil by the spring.

Now we can turn our attention to the soil. You have cared for it all season, added compost, watered it well, and do not want it to go to waste. It is the source of next year's harvest. There are a couple of approaches to take. Again, which way you go will depend on your own individual circumstances.

The first option is to simply leave the raised beds alone. Dump out the soil from any containers you grew in, adding them to the raised beds. Clean out your containers and call it a day.

The second option is much more work. I have found it successful, while others have not. So, I will leave it up to you to decide, but it seems to work for me. Find a suitable corner of your yard and empty out all the soil from all of your raised beds and growing containers into a large pile. Add to this some grass clippings or leaves as you have available and mix it all up.

In effect, you are making a large compost pile out of your soil and grass cuttings. Over the winter, if you are able and willing, then mix it up a few more times. By the time spring comes back, this soil will be rejuvenated and full of life. By mixing it all together, you reduce the impact of certain plants and pests on the soil.

Think of it as the reverse of crop rotation. As you have only a limited growing space, you are rotating the soil between the beds, instead of changing the plants you grow. Yes, you have to refill your raised bed and containers before you can get growing again, but that is a small price to pay to have happy plants. With the rotated soil in your raised beds and containers, then you can mix in your winter-aged compost and plant your seedlings.

But before we can put our seedlings in the soil, we need to talk about water.

Chapter 5:

Water Me, Baby!

Step 4: Watering and Irrigation

The nectar of life. Every living organism needs water in some form or another. Our planet, and thus us by extension, would not be the same if it weren't for water.

Your plants will come to rely on you to water them when there is not enough rainfall to do the job. Unless you are lucky enough to have an artesian spring in your backyard—and I have only ever come across one of those so far—then you will be responsible to provide healthy water to your plants as they need it.

I am sure you noticed I specified healthy water. Did you know water could be unhealthy for plants? There might be too much salt, too much soda, or too much iron. There is any number of minerals that might be in the water that we can filter out for us to drink, but unfiltered would harm or kill your plants. And I know we have all seen the news reports of chemical spills, oil spills, burning well water, and the like. The contamination of the world's drinking water is not restricted to one location. It is now found in all parts of the globe.

The same applies to plants. They need water that is clean, and free of harmful chemicals and contaminants. But unlike us, they are not as tolerant to high or low pH, incorrect mineral contents, and the overall quality of the water. It is true that if you look closely, you will find plants growing in environments that would be fatal to us, but these are very specialized plants, not the type you are going to plant in your garden and expect to eat.

What is required to nourish your garden is clean, pH-neutral water, in abundance at the right time, and location. Given the state of the world's water supply, this sounds like a difficult bill to fill, but in reality, it isn't. The vast majority of gardeners will water their plants with either their city-supplied tap water, rainwater, or a combination of the two. And the vast majority of gardens will flourish with this water supply.

Did you know that most city water supplies are typically run first through a particulate filter for sediment removal, then a series of carbon filters to eliminate any bad tastes? This clean water is now mixed with several different pH buffers to keep the water at a neutral pH of 7. This helps reduce any chemical wear in the water distribution system, increasing the life of the pipes, and reducing the delivery cost of your water.

So, what does this mean to me? You now have an endless supply of clean, safe water for your plants. The pH, set at 7 by the city, is higher than the 6.5 most plants prefer, but your plants are amazing. If grown from seedlings in pH 7 water, they will adapt and thrive.

If you are one of those that get their water from a well, dugout, or rain catchment, then the chemical composition of your water will be different than that found in the city. I would suggest that it is worth the time and expense to have your water tested at least every few years. This is the only sure way to determine that it is safe for you to drink and for your plants.

Rainwater is the perfect source to water your plants, if you have access to it, and are allowed to store it. It comes ready filtered, clean, and with a pH of 5.5 to 6. This is what plants all over the world prefer to be watered with.

So, what happens if you normally use city water as it is and don't treat it or filter it or do anything to it? Nothing. Your plants will love rainwater when they can get it when it rains, and the lower pH of the rainwater will assist in nutrient uptake. But if you have only city water to use, your plants will love this as well, it may take them a few weeks to adjust, but that's all.

The flip side of that is if your garden is located where it will be watered when it rains, then you need only worry about not flooding your beds or containers. Ensure you have adequate drainage holes in the low spots, and some way to direct this excess water away.

How to Water

With your water supply now sorted out, let's talk about actually putting the water on the plants. You can imagine that there are as many ways to do this as there are people. Some gardeners swear by hand watering with a watering can and only after sundown, while others will only ever water with a hose first thing in the morning. Still, others will insist that a watering can is a waste of time and bury extensive networks of soaker hoses in the soil. And let's not forget the tech-head who has his garden wired up to a computer. To add to the confusion, I am sure you have all seen the landscape piping, pop-up spray heads, and drippers they sell at the garden store.

So, what is the right way? The answer to that is like the answer to "how long is a piece of string?" It depends.

How often are you able, or willing to water your plants? What is the climate like where you are growing? How good is your soil? What type of plants are you growing? It gets complex, but there are a few tried and true methods that will get you started. After a few weeks of practice, and keeping a close eye on your plants, you will naturally gravitate to the system that makes the most sense to your situation, your gardening style, and your aesthetic.

Watering Cans

Watering cans. Might as well start with them. Everyone has a mental picture of that perfect watering can. Likely with a graceful, arched spout, and made from brass, copper, or some other gorgeous material. Just like the one grandma had.

I am not going to say don't use these, but they are a great deal of work for outdoor plants. You will find that as the season progresses, each plant will require more at each watering. The limitations of your watering can will be quite apparent when you have to bring two, or three, cans of water to each tomato plant. That does get tiresome pretty quickly. There is an upside to using a watering can, precise delivery of water directly to the plant stalks.

Hoses

This covers plenty of options. Many things can be attached to the end of your hose: sprinklers, watering wands, spray heads, and soaker hoses.

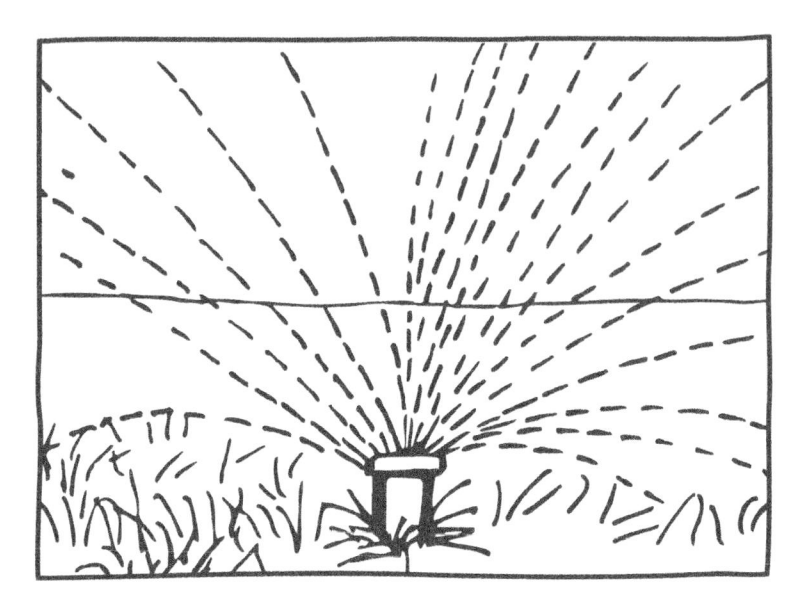

Sprinklers

Let's begin with sprinklers. What image just popped into your head? Some laughing, happy kids running through the sprinkler on the lawn? It is a hot summer day, and everyone is smiling and enjoying themselves. The ideal bucolic childhood memory, true or created.

Perfection for sure, but not for your plants. Sprinklers were designed to water grass—large, open expanses of grass—and they do that magnificently. But think about your raised beds and containers. There is no way the sprinkler can tell the difference between them and the lawn or patio beneath them. They will over-spray your plants, and all that extra water costs you money. Not the wisest choice.

Watering Wands

Watering wands. I've seen these advertised as the new watering can. They have the same rainfall head to softly distribute the water like an old-fashioned watering can.

Combine this with an endless supply of water and it seems like a no-brainer for the best choice.

Almost. If you have a watering wand that is long enough for you to reach the stalks of the plants, through the foliage, then you are getting close. The typical watering wand is too short, forcing you to top water your plants. But wait, what is wrong with that? Rain top waters everything.

That is a true statement, however, most of the edible varieties you are likely to grow in your garden tend to be susceptible to mould and mildew. Top watering creates the perfect environment for powdery mildew to flourish, among other things. Unless you also happen to grow in a location with lots of wind, which will bring its own issues, then I would recommend you stay away from top watering.

So, you have a long watering wand and want to get busy watering. Go for it, just watch out for your hose. I cannot count the number of times I have dragged my hose across the garden, only to look back and see I have crushed a tomato plant or my basil. Frustrating to say the least. When using a watering wand as your primary watering tool, I would suggest you either pay a great deal of attention to the hose behind you, or use several smaller hoses set up at different locations in the garden area.

Spray Heads

Spray heads. You know, those pistol-grip jobs you use to wash your car, clean out the gutters, and occasionally soak your spouse. Yeah, I saw that smile. These are great for some uses, but like a short watering wand, they force you to top water your plants. So, keep them aside for your car and those cheeky fun days in the summer.

Soaker Hoses

Soaker hoses. If you don't know what I mean by this, I am referring to a couple of styles of hoses that leak water. Some have hundreds of small pin holes in them, while others are made from a plastic that seeps water.

Typically, you would either bury these in your soil before you planted your seedlings or lay them under your mulch, weaving the hose in such a manner that each plant will get some of the water.

Soaker hoses work wonderfully, if you remember to turn them on when needed and maybe more importantly, off when done. If you are planning to use soaker hoses, I would recommend attaching a timer to the end of it. This will allow you to time the watering to best suit your schedule and ensure it is turned off after the correct amount of time. It is a very bad day to go into your garden and find a raised bed transformed into a swimming pool. Not only have you most likely drowned all your plants, but you have also spent a great deal of money on the water to do so.

If none of these appeal to you, there are still more options, though you will need to be a tad handy with tools.

Automated Watering

This is a very broad topic, ranging all the way from the simple elegance of terracotta, all the way up to computer-controlled, sensor-driven masterpieces that could control a city. Obviously, we are going to stay at the simple, inexpensive end of this spectrum, but if you are the type that enjoys creating a complex system that will water your plants when needed, then I wish you the best of luck and look forward to seeing your creation on your socials.

This is where your creativity can shine once again. I have no doubt that once you have gardened for a season or two, you will have your own amazing ways to automate your plant watering. I am going to go through a few examples to get you started.

Terracotta Pots

Using terracotta pots is about as simple as it gets. All you need to do is seal the hole in the bottom of the pot with epoxy, heavy-duty tape, or something similar as long as the hole does not leak. Next, you need to dig away the soil near your plant and bury the terracotta pot almost flush with the soil. These work best when you water the surrounding soil first, and then fill the terracotta pot with water.

Terracotta is water-permeable. This means that water will slowly seep out of the pot and into the surrounding soil. All you need to do is keep the pot full, and it will water the plants nearby. You will have to adjust the number, and size of these pots depending on your soil, the size of your growing space, and how much water your plants require. Terracotta pots may not replace your normal watering methods, but they will help keep the soil moisture levels consistent, and possibly give you a day or two off if you want a short vacation.

Self-Watering Pots

The next way to automate your watering is also a simple one, though it will require a bit more construction than filling a hole and burying a pot.

A self-watering pot, a staple in the hydroponics world, is a very effective method to water your plants and requires only occasional intervention from you. The one drawback to this is it will only work in a container. To set this up for a raised bed would be too expensive to justify the effort.

Let me explain the theory a little before we head out and start building. A self-watering pot is basically two of the same pots nestled together with an air space left in the bottom pot. If they are too tight, then you will need to put a spacer in the bottom pot to create an empty space. This is the water reservoir that will sustain the plant in the pot above.

Now, we know that soil can wick water up, sideways, and away from the source. We are going to take advantage of this property by using a small container of soil hung from the top bucket, and immersed in the water, to wick moisture up from the reservoir and into the top bucket.

So, how do we make this contraption?

It is much simpler than it sounds. Firstly, we need a container that your growing container will fit inside. It can be a tight fit, or loose enough that your growing container will sit in the middle of the other one and not touch the sides. Whatever you can find. Now, using some stones, or bricks, something that won't rust or rot ideally, create a raised area for your pot to sit on.

This next step can be done after you have planted in your pot, but it is easier to do this before you fill it with dirt. You are going to need a short plastic container, like a yogurt or plastic takeaway. You need to cut out a hole in the bottom of the top pot, such that the plastic container will fit, but not fall through. Before you fill it with soil, make a bunch of holes in the small plastic container. Now push it into the hole and fill the entire lot with soil.

Once you place the upper container into the lower one and fill the water level up past the bottom of the top container, the water will wick up through your yogurt container and into the top pot.

After a day or two, the soil in the top pot will be moist, perfect for your plants. As your plants grow, they will draw as much water as they require up through the yogurt container, so all you need is to keep the lower container filled with water to the correct level. You will be amazed how well your plants grow with water on demand like this, and it can give you some time off to enjoy your summer.

Drip Irrigation

This is all about pumps, timers, and computers. In the most basic form, this is a water supply, which could be your city-supplied water, a timer, and pipes that run out to each plant and deliver the water through a calibrated drip head or micro spray head.

For a basic drip irrigation system, as any more detail than this will require a site visit to look around your garden, you will need a water supply. If you choose to connect to your city water, then make sure you have double shut-off timers on the hose. The last thing you need is to flood your yard when one timer malfunctions. Once you have a water supply, the next piece of information you need is the water requirements of your plants, and to figure out if you are dripping on each plant or using a micro spray head to water a larger section of your raised beds.

With this determined, you then need to run a large hose to each raised bed, and then smaller branch hoses to each dripper or micro sprinkler. The way the system works is the hose timer turns on the water, which runs through the pipes and to the drippers and micro-sprinklers. Irrigation drippers come in several calibrated options, with one, two, or four litres an hour being the common ones. The same applies to micro sprinkler heads. So, now that you have water at each plant, all you need to do is set the timer to run long enough to deliver the correct amount of water to each plant. Sounds pretty simple, doesn't it? It is. The main hurdles are the cost of setting up the system and maintaining it.

Some people love this approach to watering, as it gives them precise control and can run unattended for an entire week or more. But this is a much more complex, and thus expensive way to water your plants.

When to Water

If you want to get gardeners talking, then ask them, "When is the best time to water your plants?" Everyone has a different opinion as to why their timing is the best. And of course, they will have endless horror stories to debunk everyone else's ideas. Keep this in mind as we head into this tricky topic. As you get experience you will find your own watering routine that works for you. All I can do is suggest a few ideas that will help you get started.

"Early morning is the best."

If you are a morning person, then that is brilliant. Get out and water all your plants before the morning dew is gone. For the rest of us, we are more likely to come out mid-morning, once the sun is actually up. This too works as a good time to water.

"Never water in the afternoon."

Some people adhere to this at all costs, but if you work shift work and are just getting up, or about to go to sleep, and this is when you have time to water, then this is the perfect time to water your plants.

"Only ever water at night."

Yeah, I've heard that as well. If you have a day job like most of us, and you are unable to get out to your garden until the evening, then this is also the perfect time to water your plants.

You can see what I am getting at. Whatever schedule you have will work for your plants. They are forgiving and adaptable. Just make sure you remember to water them.

Where to Water

Plants need water. This is something we can all agree on. But where to water them is a topic of much debate. The arguments go like this: Top watering simulates natural rainfall and is the best for plants. Watering under the leaves keeps the foliage dry, reducing the chance of mildew and moulds. Bottom watering through the soil keeps the crust of the soil dry, preventing weeds and soil borne pests.

All of these arguments have a valid point in them. I have known gardeners that will only ever water the way they feel is best, and they have successful gardens. I have also known gardeners that water however they feel, whenever they feel, and they have also had successful gardens.

The advice I can give to clear these muddy waters is to water close to the plant in need, water a sufficient amount, and monitor for pests and moulds. If you find problems, maybe alter how you water. I know this is all a bit vague, but plant care is more what works for you, than some precise plant care regime. Your plants will adapt to your style, and flourish. Learn to enjoy the experience of figuring out what your plants need, you will have a much better connection to them, and care for them better than if I stated a watering plan you must follow. Gardening is a personal experience and through your interactions with your plants, not only will they grow and flourish, but as well will you.

Chapter 6:

Time to Get Dirty!

Step 5: Planting

In the words of Christina Aguilera, "If you ain't dirty, you ain't here to party."

We have your raised bed and containers all ready to go. You have some water and have prepared your soil. Now what? Put your seedlings, or seeds, into the soil. I know you have seen those endless racks of seeds at your local shops and are wondering if you can, or should, use these.

There are several advantages to using seeds. They are cheaper, you can select the specific variety of plant you want to grow, and they will store for a couple years, saving you money next year as well. If you are well-organized and can start to germinate your seeds early enough to have them ready for spring planting, then seeds are an ideal choice. However, purchasing pre grown seedlings requires less planning and growing time before they can be planted outside.

Indoor Seed Starting

Here is a quick guide to starting your seeds indoors and growing them up to the seedling size you can purchase at your garden store.

Steps	Details
Prepare a well-lighted starting area	To start your seeds, you need a warm area that will hold a tray or other suitable container. You will need a couple grow lights and a timer set to 14 hours on and 10 hours off.
Find your tray or containers	Seeds will germinate in almost anything, provided they have some moisture and light. A simple medium to use is old newspapers or several layers of paper towels. You can also use potting soil from the garden store if you want.

Prepare the seeds	Rinse your seeds to moisten them and place them on the surface of your chosen media and cover with either several layers of paper towel or newspaper or a finger's depth of soil. Moisten soil or media with a spray bottle.
Watch and wait	Keep a close eye on your seeds and keep the cover media moist. Most seeds will germinate within a week or two.
Thin the plants	As the seeds emerge, remove any that are weak and slow growing, keeping only the strongest.
Transplant	Once the seedlings have several leaves, very, very carefully remove them from your media and plant them in a small pot filled with soil, either potting soil or soil from your garden.
Let them grow	Keep your seedlings watered and under the grow lights until they are several inches tall.
Harden Off	When outside temperatures have warmed up, place your seedlings outside during the day, returning them to the seeding area by night. Continue to do this for a couple weeks until the local nighttime temperatures stay warm.
Move outside	Now that your plants are hardened off, it is time to move your seedlings out into their new homes.

Direct Sowing

Not every plant you want to grow needs to be started indoors. Many varieties will happily germinate and grow outside in your raised beds or containers. By selecting these plants, you not only save yourself all the work of looking after the seeds inside, you also ensure that the seedlings are adapted and happy with your local growing conditions.

Direct sowing is simply planting your seeds in either a hole, or a row, in their final garden location. Your seed packages will specify the spacing between seeds and the depth below the soil surface.

The most common vegetables to direct sow are:

- Beans
- Beets
- Carrots

- Corn
- Cucumbers
- Lettuce
- Peas
- Pumpkins
- Radishes
- Spinach
- Spring Onions
- Swiss Chard
- Turnips

Depending on where you live, and the time of year, different plants are ready to be planted. The following tables give a summary of the most common herbs, fruits, and vegetables to be planted.

Season	Location	Plant	
Summer	Subtropical—Southeast QLD and Northern NSW	Herbs	Basil, chives, coriander, lemongrass, mint, parsley
		Fruit and Vegetables	Artichoke, beans, capsicum, celery, cabbage, cucumber, eggplant, leek, lettuce, melons, onion, potato, squash, tomato

Wet and Dry Tropical—North QLD, NT, WA	Herbs	Basil, coriander, lemongrass, mint
	Fruit and Vegetables	Artichoke, beet, capsicum, cauliflower, celery, cabbage, cucumber, eggplant, lettuce, pumpkins, tomato
Dry Inland—Arid or Outback	Herbs	Too Hot
	Fruit and Vegetables	Too Hot
Temperate Areas—Sydney, coastal NSW, Victoria	Herbs	Basil, chives, coriander, fennel, mint, parsley
	Fruit and vegetables	Beans, beet, broccoli, cabbage, capsicum, carrot, cauliflower, celery, chili, cabbage, cucumber, eggplant, leek, lettuce, parsnip, potato, corn, sweet potato, zucchini
Cool/Southern Tablelands—Melbourne, Tasmania	Herbs	Basil, chives, coriander, lemongrass, mint, oregano, parsley, rosemary, thyme

		Fruit and vegetables	Beans, beet, cabbage, capsicum, carrot, cauliflower, cucumber, spinach, leek, lettuce, onion, parsnip, pumpkin, radish, squash, corn, tomato
	Mediterranean—Adelaide, Perth	Herbs	Care only
		Fruits and vegetables	Capsicum, tomatoes, zucchini,

Season	Location	Plant	
Autumn	Subtropical—Southeast QLD and Northern NSW	Herbs	Chervil, chicory, fennel, garlic, oregano, parsley
		Fruit and Vegetables	Beans, broccoli, lettuce, onion, peas, radishes, spinach, turnip
	Wet and Dry Tropical—North QLD, NT, WA	Herbs	Basil, coriander, garlic, chives, oregano, parsley, thyme
		Fruit and Vegetables	Beans, beet, broccoli, cabbage, capsicum, carrot, cauliflower, celery, cabbage, cucumber, eggplant, lettuce,

			melons, onion, parsnip. Potato, pumpkin, squash, corn, tomato
	Dry Inland—Arid or Outback	Herbs	Chervil, chives, coriander, dill, fennel, garlic, mint, oregano, parsley, rosemary, thyme
		Fruit and Vegetables	Beans, broccoli, cauliflower, lettuce, onion, peas, spinach, tomato
	Temperate Areas—Sydney, coastal NSW, Victoria	Herbs	Coriander, garlic, oregano, parsley, thyme
		Fruit and vegetables	Beans, spinach, peas
	Cool/Southern Tablelands—Melbourne, Tasmania	Herbs	Chives, coriander, garlic, lemongrass, mint, oregano, parsley, thyme
		Fruit and vegetables	Broad bean, beet, cabbage, carrot, cauliflower, broccoli, cabbage, spinach, leek, lettuce, onion, parsnip, potato, turnip
	Mediterranean—Adelaide, Perth	Herbs	Chives, oregano, parsley

		Fruits and vegetables	Citrus, avocado, broccoli, cabbage, beans, cauliflower, celery, spinach, lettuce, peas

Season	Location	Plant	
Winter	Subtropical—Southeast QLD and Northern NSW	Herbs	Chamomile, cress, dill, garlic, mint, oregano, parsley, thyme
		Fruit and Vegetables	Beet, cabbage, onions, carrots, tomato, lettuce
	Wet and Dry Tropical—North QLD, NT, WA	Herbs	Dill, garlic, mint, oregano, parsley, rocket, thyme
		Fruit and Vegetables	Beans, broccoli, cabbage, capsicum, carrot, cauliflower, cucumber, eggplant, lettuce, potato, pumpkin, corn, tomato
	Dry Inland—Arid or Outback	Herbs	Too Hot
		Fruit and Vegetables	Artichoke, asparagus, beans, beet, broccoli, cabbage, carrot, lettuce, onion,

		potato, peas, pumpkin, spinach
Temperate Areas—Sydney, coastal NSW, Victoria	Herbs	Chamomile, coriander, cress, dill, garlic, mint, oregano, parsley, thyme
	Fruit and vegetables	Asparagus, bean, cabbage, cauliflower, onions, spinach
Cool/Southern Tablelands—Melbourne, Tasmania	Herbs	Chives, cress, dill, mint, parsley, thyme
	Fruit and vegetables	Artichoke, asparagus, beet, bean, broccoli, cabbage, carrot, cauliflower, celery, leek, lettuce, onion, peas, spinach
Mediterranean—Adelaide, Perth	Herbs	Cress, parsley
	Fruits and vegetables	Artichoke, asparagus, bean, cabbage, carrot, cauliflower, spinach, lettuce, onion, pea

Season	Location	Plant	
Spring	Subtropical—Southeast QLD and Northern NSW	Herbs	Basil, chives, coriander, dill, mint, oregano, parsley, thyme
		Fruit and Vegetables	Beans, beet, broccoli, cabbage, capsicum, carrot, cabbage, cucumber, eggplant, squash, lettuce, onion, potato, corn, potato, tomato
	Wet and Dry Tropical—North QLD, NT, WA	Herbs	Basil, chili, chives, dill, mint oregano, parsley
		Fruit and Vegetables	Beet, capsicum, carrot, cabbage, corn, cucumber, eggplant, lettuce, onion, spinach, potato, tomato
	Dry Inland—Arid or Outback	Herbs	Protect from heat
		Fruit and Vegetables	Beans, capsicum, onion, corn
	Temperate Areas—Sydney, coastal NSW, Victoria	Herbs	Basil, chives, coriander, dill, mint, oregano, parsley, thyme

		Fruit and vegetables	Beans, beet, broccoli, cabbage, capsicum, cucumber, eggplant, lettuce, onion, potato, pumpkin, squash, corn, tomato
	Cool/Southern Tablelands - Melbourne, Tasmania	Herbs	Basil, chives, coriander, dill, mint, oregano, parsley, thyme
		Fruit and vegetables	Beet, broccoli, cabbage, capsicum, carrot, celery, cucumber, eggplant, lettuce, onion, pea, spinach, corn, tomato
	Mediterranean— Adelaide, Perth	Herbs	Basil, chives, coriander, dill, mint, oregano, parsley, thyme
		Fruits and vegetables	Broccoli, carrot, celery, cucumber, lettuce, beet, pea, spinach, corn, tomato

Companion Planting

Like you and your crew of closest mates, plants do better with certain other plants around. This is called companion planting. The benefits range from providing nutrients in the soil, shade to prevent sunburn, attracting pollinators, or repelling insects and pests.

There are a few common approaches to companion planting: attract beneficial predators and pollinators, repel pests with flowers, and smothering out weeds.

Attracting pollinators and beneficial insects will not only increase your garden yield, but it will also reduce the stress on your plants which will make them healthier and more productive. Interplanting your edible food plants with calendula or cosmos will attract pollinators directly to your plants. These insects not only pollinate your plants, but most of them love the taste of aphids.

Repelling pests works on the opposite principle. Choose a plant that you like the look of, but that insects do not. *Nasturtiums* and marigolds do double duty: They look great, and attract not only pollinators and aphids, making a perfect buffet for all those good insects buzzing around.

The final approach is to cover exposed soil with a dense planting of ground cover plants. Marigolds, poached egg plants, or clover will spread out and cover any unplanted soil. Not only will they help keep moisture evaporation down and function as living mulch to keep weeds from germinating, they will also attract pollinators, and repel detrimental insects.

Common companion plants that will help increase your harvest and reduce your workload.

- *Calendula*
- Marigold
- Chamomile
- Daisy
- Poached Egg Plant

- Onions
- Garlic
- Comfrey
- *Nasturtium*
- *Phacelia*
- Buckwheat
- Clover

So, be kind, and give your plants some friends. They will thank you come harvest time.

Be My Pollinator!

"Where wise actions are the fruit of life, wise discourse is the pollination." — Bryant H. McGill

We won't talk about pollinators until Chapter 8, but rest assured, these little guys are key to a successful raised bed garden.

Pollinator Partnership says that pollinating animals are responsible for one in every three mouthfuls of the food we consume, simply because they travel between plants with pollen. This is how our plants reproduce – and the process is essential to a thriving and self-sustaining garden.

To learn more about how to attract pollinators to your garden, you'll need to keep reading, but suffice to say that they are enticed by the colors of a plant's flower, and rewarded by the nectar it brings them.

In essence, they're much like us – we visit a place that attracts us for some reason and brings us a reward, be that entertainment, information, or sustenance. That's why you're reading this book – you were attracted by the promise of learning more about raised bed gardening, and your reward will be the food you're going to be able to produce with the new knowledge you've acquired.

To take this metaphor a step further, I'd like to ask you to become a pollinator yourself, spreading your wings to take the information to other gardeners.

Don't worry – it's a lot easier than it sounds. All I'd like you to do is take a few minutes to leave a review.

<u>By leaving a review of this book on Amazon, you'll show new readers where they can find the raised bed gardening advice they need to grow delicious food for their families.</u>

Simply by letting other readers know how this book has helped you and what they'll find inside, you'll show them where they can find the information they're looking for to get started on their own gardening journey.

Thank you for rolling with my metaphor… Keep reading to find out what you can do to make the most of the pollinators in your garden, and thank you for taking the time to help out a fellow gardener.

Chapter 7:

Growing, Growing, Harvested!

Step 6: Maintaining Your Money-Saving Crops

All your seedlings from seeds have been transplanted out into your raised beds. Your store-bought seedlings have been planted. What's next? Now you get to look after your new charges. Caring for your plants, and helping them create a lush, abundant garden is one of life's unexpected joys, until you have done it that is.

With a gentle, understanding touch, you will help transform all those delicate seedlings into your salad, dinner, or preserve that will last the winter.

Care

There are countless ways to look after your plants, but I am going to present here the most common, and hopefully, most effective steps to follow from transplanting through to harvest.

- Mulch
    - With your seedlings established in their new locations, cover the remaining exposed soil with an organic mulch. This will assist in weed control and help maintain optimal moisture levels in the soil.

- Water
    - Water your plants regularly. Start with pushing your finger deep into the soil. Is it damp? You do not need to water. If it is dry, then water. Over

the next few weeks, you will learn how much and how often your plants will need water. Remember this will change over the season.

- Weeding

    o Remove all weeds as soon as they appear. They will compete with your seedlings for water and nutrients and potentially stunt the growth of your chosen plants.

- Fertilize

    o If you have an established compost, an occasional light top dressing of well-aged compost will give your plants a nutrient boost. But do not overdo it. Too much compost will burn your plants instead of helping them.

- Remove the Dead

    o As your plants grow, some will die. It is just the nature of gardening. Remove the dead plants and add to your compost. This will remove any potential pest attractant or mould source.

- Supports

    o As your plants grow, some will need a helping hand. Make sure to provide sticks, trellises, or other types of support to keep your plant upright and happy.

- Clean Tools

    o   After each day's use of your tools, if you are digging out weeds, trimming dead shoots, or harvesting produce, then make sure to clean your tools before your next use. This will reduce the chance of spreading any unknown pest or disease throughout your garden.

- Prune

    o   As your plants grow, you may find shoots and branches that have no produce on them. Depending on the plant, you should remove these unproductive areas so the plant can concentrate on ripening the existing produce.

- Space

    o   If you misjudged the planting space requirements when you seeded your garden, then as your plants grow you may need to thin them out. Remove any of the crowded or weak plants to create enough space for the rest to thrive.

- Harvest

    o   As your produce ripens, ensure you harvest it promptly. Any fruit, or vegetables left behind may begin to rot, and affect the productivity of the plant. Harvesting ripe produce will also allow the plants to put more energy into ripening the remaining produce before the growing season comes to an end.

- End of Season Work
  - Once all your harvest is picked, you still have some work to do. Pull out the stalks of any annual plant and add them to your compost. Remove any other unwanted debris from your raised beds and cover the soil with a layer of compost. Everything is now ready to start again once the weather warms up enough next year.

Next Year

Over the winter, as you enjoy the fruits of your summer's work, you can begin to plan your next garden. You will have learned what plants grow well in your location, and under your care. Working with this information, you can create your next layout and seeding schedule. But before you get too detailed and carried away designing the perfect raised-bed garden, we need to talk about crop rotation.

Now, I expect you've heard the term, but think that it only applies to large farm operations. While they might be growing a million stalks of corn, and you are only growing eight, the principle is the same.

Each different plant will extort a different ratio of nutrients from the soil each growing season. Eventually this imbalance will become extreme enough that those plants will be unable to grow in that soil.

There are two common solutions to this issue. First is to add complex fertilizers that contain the missing nutrients, but this a very expensive option, and as a backyard grower it is unlikely you will have access to these commercial products.

But don't worry. The other method to address this nutrient imbalance is free. All you need to do is change the growing location of your plants every year. No, I don't mean you need to move your raised beds around the back yard. You just need to plant each plant in a different area of the raised beds.

Another advantage of rotating your crops is pest control. With some pests living in the top layer of the soil, when you move your plants, there is little to no food for these pests, and their numbers should decrease.

The typical rotation schedule is in the following chart, though your garden may vary depending on the specific plant varieties you are growing. To use this chart, find your plant, and the column to the right will tell you where to move it next season. Plants in the last column move into the location of plants in the first column.

Year 1	Year 2	Year 3	Year 4
Tomato, Basil, Capsicum, Pumpkin	Bean, Cucumber, Squash, Lettuce	Carrot, Onion, Broccoli, Swiss Chard, Potato	Pea, Leek, Beet, Eggplant, Radish

To follow this rotation schedule, ideally you would be growing in four raised-bed gardens.

Chapter 8:

Besties or Frenemies? What You Need to Know About Beneficial Bugs and Pesky Pests

We need to talk about insects. And yes, there are good insects as well. So why do we want beneficial insects in our garden?

They serve a variety of roles, but the primary ones are either pollination or pest control.

Pollination

The vast majority of the food supply for the plant relies on insects to pollinate the flowers that, in turn, allows the plant to grow the produce we eat. While there are GMO varieties of tomatoes, for example, that can self-pollinate, any of the varieties of plants you are likely to grow in your raised beds will need the assistance of pollinating insects to produce edible items.

If you have ever been in a healthy garden at the height of summer, you likely noticed all the flying insects competing with you for time at each plant. These are the pollinators. Bees, flies, wasps, and butterflies are very obvious as they flit between plants and investigate every single open flower.

It is the other pollinators that you are unlikely to spot, unless you have a very keen eye and know what to look for. I am talking about beetles and ants. These ground dwellers are not interested in the pollen or nectar but are focused on food. They are hunting aphids and other plant pests, and in the process, will help pollinate your plants.

So, with this in mind, you can understand the importance of pesticide and herbicide use. If you kill off all the pollinators when you spray for weed control, then you will have a very beautiful garden and very little to harvest.

Pest Control

While flower pollination is essential, it is when we use insects to help control our garden pests that we begin to appreciate them. We've all seen the nature films, so I don't need to go into any detail. Hungry insects are your friends, and it turns out very, very few of them are vegetarians. But how do I tell them apart? What is a good insect and what is a pest?

These are very good questions. We are going to start with the beneficial insects, partly because there are fewer of them, and you want to see these in your garden. If you spot an insect that is not on this list, then there is a very good chance it is one you do not want hanging around your plants.

Good Insects

Here are 18 of the most common good insects and some information on them to help you identify and understand why they are good to have around.

Insect	Range	Description	Why We Like Them
Bumblebee	Worldwide	Big, lazy, clumsy, black and yellow bees.	Pollinator
Burying Beetle	Cooler Climates	About 3 cm long, black and with orange banding	They bury dead insects under the soil providing nutrients for your plants.

103

Butterfly	Worldwide	Numerous colors and patterns	Pollinator
Centipede	Worldwide	Multi-legged, worm-like creatures	Pest control. They eat aphids, slugs, snails, and cutworms
Damselfly	Worldwide	Looks like a small delicate dragonfly	Pest control, eating mosquitos and other flying insects
Dragonfly	Worldwide	Large, multi-winged, flying insect	Pest control, eating flies and mosquitos
Earthworm	Worldwide	Soil-dwelling worm	Aerate soil and provide nutrients for plants.
Honeybee	Worldwide	Up to 1.5 cm long, agile, numerous colors and patterns	Pollinator
Lacewing	Worldwide	Flying insect with green or brown lace like wings	Pest control, eating aphids, whitefly, and caterpillars
Ladybug	Worldwide	Half-round with red or orange shell with black or grey spots	Pest control, eating aphids and whitefly

| Spiders | Worldwide | Eight-legged insect | Pest control, eating most insects. Some varieties may be harmful to humans. |

Best Plants to Attract Good Insects

Now that you know which good bugs you want in your garden, how do you get them there? You bribe them. By planting the correct plants, these good insects will be unable to resist the allure of your garden. At least that is the theory. Like people, insects prefer different types of plants, so it makes sense for us to plant a variety of insect-attractive plants and try to persuade as many as possible to come over.

The most common plants used in gardens are listed here along with the good bugs they tend to attract.

Plant	Beneficial Insects
Bachelor Buttons	Ladybugs, Lacewings, Beetles
Cleome	Butterflies, Bees
Cosmos	Butterflies, Bees
Black-Eyed Susan	Butterflies, Bees, Beetles
Daisy	Bees, Lacewings
Marigold	Ladybugs
Nasturtium	Butterflies, Bees
Purple Coneflower	Butterflies, Bees
Salvia	Butterflies, Bees, Hummingbirds
Sunflower	Beetles, Bees, Butterflies, Spiders
Yarrow	Butterflies, Bees
Zinnia	Butterflies

So, now that we have our raised beds full of good insects, we should figure out how to discourage the pests from arriving. Depending on where you live and garden, then you will have different common pests, but the following table will allow you to identify and discourage the most common garden pests.

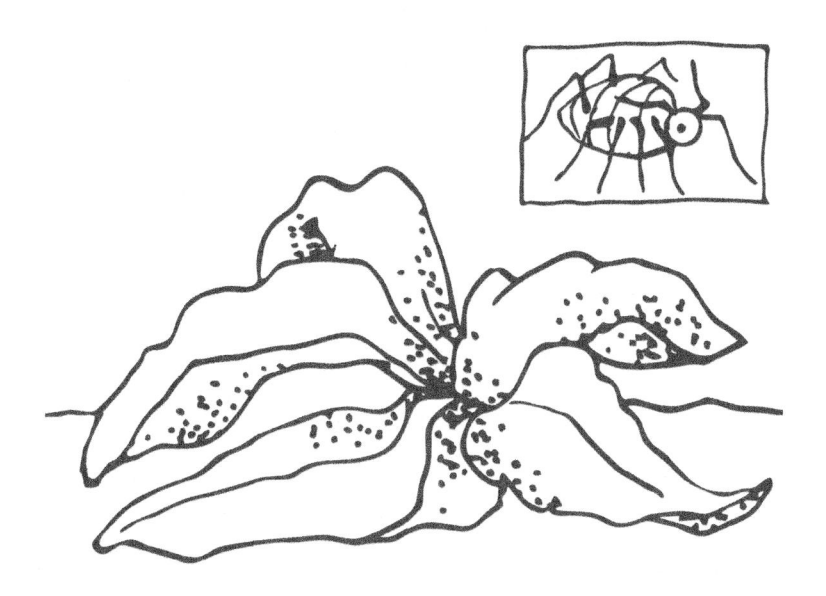

Pest Insect Identification

Pest	Symptoms of Infestation	Control Measures
Aphids	Sticky substance coating leaves and stalks. Stunted growth, curled leaves that are yellowing or turning brown.	Prune the affected portions of the plant. Spray with pressure water to dislodge. Apply tomato leaf or garlic spray or attract ladybugs, beetles, or lacewings.
African Black Beetle	Wilted potato stems and damaged potatoes. Foliage turns red or yellow and possible sprouting at the base of the plant stalk due to damage.	Dig in a plastic barrier around the plants at least five centimetres deep into the soil. Use domestic birds like chickens to reduce beetle population.

Australian Plague Locust	Red legged, and black wingtips on a grasshopper 25 to 44 cm long.	Add plant covers, hand pick, and remove.
Azalea Lace Bug	Living on the underside of leaves and growing no more than 6 mm long. Damaged leaves will be bleached or bronze in color.	Pressure water to dislodge, attract lacewings, ladybugs, or assassin bugs. Spray with neem oil.
Bronze Orange Bug	Orange or bronze colored beetle type bugs up to 25 mm long. Also known as a stink bug.	Hand remove bugs, or spray with neem oil, or soapy water.
Cabbage Moth/Cabbage White Butterfly	White butterflies with a wingspan up to 44 mm, while moths are greyish and up to 10 mm long. Large holes eaten in the leaves of *Brassicas*.	Remove by hand, plant herbs like dill, basil, fennel to discourage, apply *Bacillus thuringiensis* organic bio-insecticide.
Christmas Beetle	Yellow brown to red brown shiny beetles between 25 and 30 mm long that cause jagged rips in plant leaves.	Remove with pressure water.
Citrus Gall Wasp	Shiny black 3mm long wasps.	Remove the affected plant section, hang yellow sticky traps.

Citrus Leafminer	Silver white moth is around 5 mm long. Larvae will produce silver trails behind them as they eat the foliage.	Remove the affected plant portion, spray with neem oil, and attract lacewings.
Codling Moth	Small grey moth about 1 cm long. Leaves holes in fruit.	Spray with a mix of white oil and water, attract ladybugs, and lacewings.
European Earwig	Up to 25 mm long and are nocturnal. Jagged leaf edges and holes. Damage is similar to snails and slugs.	Trap with linseed oil or beer.
Fruit Fly	Small flies leave maggots in fruit to mature.	Use chickens to help control pest population, use pheromone-based traps.
Grasshoppers	Similar to locusts but smaller	Hand remove, cover plants, use chickens for pest control
Hibiscus Beetle	Tiny, at 3 mm long. Feeds on unopened flowers.	Spray with water and soap mixture.
Mealybug	Waxy, white bug about 4 mm long. Leaves will yellow, plants will wilt, and foliage will be sticky.	Use pressure water to remove, attract ladybugs and lacewings, or spray bugs with alcohol or neem oil.

Millipedes	Up to 50 mm long, with four legs per segment, they may eat new seedlings.	Spray with neem oil or hand pick.
Psyllids	Small, white and about 4 mm in size. Cause early leaf drop, yellowed leaves, or fatal dieback of the plant.	Attract ladybugs and lacewings, spray with neem oil.
Root-Knot Nematodes	Root bound roundworms too small to be seen by the naked eye. Cause wilting and yellowing.	Remove infected plants and crop rotation for next season.
Scale Insects	Waxy covered insects from 1 to 5 mm in length. Dieback of plants and distorted fruit.	Remove infested plants, spray with neem oil, attract ladybugs and lacewings.
Slaters	Small, armored pill bugs. May kill young seedlings.	Trap.
Snails and Slugs	With or without a shell. Damaged leaves, dead seedlings, and silver mucus trails.	Hand remove, spray with strong coffee, use copper around raised beds.
Spider Mites	Small, red spiders that quickly overwhelm a plant. Spotted leaves and	Attract ladybugs and lacewings, use pressure water to remove, prune affected plant sections.

	plants covered in webs.	
Thrips	Black to white thin insect up to 15 mm long. Deformed leaves, stunted growth, browned leaves and early petal drop.	Attract ladybugs and lacewings, spray with neem oil, use yellow sticky traps.
Tree Borers	Unusual small holes in tree bark.	Prune affected plant sections, remove infested plants.
Weevils	Scalloped leaf edges, plant dieback, and stalks covered in small insects.	Hand remove, cover crops, spray with soapy water.
White Curl Grubs	White grub up to 40 mm long. Stunted or dead plants, unusually slow plant development.	Spray with soap and water, attract birds to your garden.
Whitefly	Look like small moths living on the underside of the leaves. Stunted growth, wilting, and yellowed leaves.	Pressure water to remove. Use yellow sticky traps, spray with neem oil.

Larger Pests

So, that more or less covered all the small creepy crawlers. Next, we need to address the larger, usually more intelligent intruders that will damage your garden. I am talking about cats, chickens, possums, and any other larger animals common to your urban environments. I am going to focus on cats and chickens, as they are the most visible and annoying.

Cats

Love them or hate them, we have to admit that cats are now part of the fabric of society. You may not have a cat sharing your house, but I expect your neighbor does, or someone on your block.

Now, I happen to like chihuahuas, so I have two. I find that this does make a great deterrent to keep away the cats on my block.

Cats are creatures of habit. If they find a nice soft garden bed that they can use as a toilet, then they will return every time the need arises. Knowing this gives you an advantage. All you need to do is either keep them away to start or make it so unpleasant that they do not want to come back.

So, how do you do this? There are few things cats hate more than water and getting tangled up in something. If you happen to spot the cat coming into your yard, spray it with your hose, but don't fall into the temptation to shout at it and scare it away. They are smart enough to connect the fright with you, and not the garden. And it then becomes a game for them: How to use your garden as a toilet, while keeping away from you. Not the best outcome.

Try to befriend the cat but spray it with the hose when it steps into your garden. The garden has now become a scary place, and hopefully it will decide to leave and head over to the park or somewhere else that has open soil.

If you look about on the internet or your local hardware stores, you will be able to find motion activated sprinkler heads. These have proven to be very effective at cat control, so long as you keep moving them about. It is the element of surprise that will finally convince the cat to move along.

However, if they insist on returning, then the other solution that I have used with good success is to place a plastic or wire mesh—like chicken wire or something with smaller holes in it—over the soil in the raised bed or container. By carefully cutting away the spaces needed by your plants and securing the mesh down with something heavy like a rock or landscape staples, the cat is unable to dig up the soil. I found that after a couple failed attempts, the cat moved along. I did keep the mesh covering the soil until harvest as a deterrent.

You might think if you have a dog that this would help. Sometimes it does, like with my two chihuahuas mentioned earlier. But cats can be smart and patient creatures, either befriending the dog, or waiting until it is out for a walk.

Some people have had success with lining the perimeter of their gardens with used coffee grounds, chili peppers, and even hanging wind chimes. I am guessing the success of these will depend on the cats in your area. One final suggestion to try, if all else fails and the cat keeps coming back, is to create a garden area that you leave for it. At least then you know where the toilet is.

Cats can be a frustrating challenge, so I wish you the best in your fight.

Chickens

Now, chickens are much simpler to manage. Typically, you are only looking to control your own flock. They tend not to wander down the block like cats.

If you have your own flock of chickens, then all you need is to either keep them in a cage or movable structure like a chicken tractor or surround your raised beds and containers with a chicken wire fence.

If you keep an eye on your chickens for a week or two, you will see how they are going after your plants, and you should have no trouble in keeping them out of your raised beds and containers.

Possums and Their Friends

Now, I will not be able to uncover the deterrents needed for every possible medium, large, or extra-large pest that may come to disturb your plants. Some creativity will be required on your part, but this might be the perfect opportunity to introduce yourself to your neighbors and their pets.

Both cats and possums respond poorly to being shouted at or sprayed with water. This soon becomes nothing more than a game to them, with you being the undesirable thing to avoid and not your garden.

To try and make the garden unpleasant, without harming them, can be a challenge, but some of the more successful options include leaving moth balls about your garden, as the smell is unpleasant to them. You can try to spray bleach or other ammonia-based cleaners on the pathways through your garden, but do this sparingly, as the bleach will harm your plants. The same applies to fish oil, hot chili oil, garlic oil, and even tea.

If you are a tech person, you could set up a motion-activated sprinkler head that you turn on at night. This should work well unless you have your own pets that like to be outside after dark.

The best advice is to keep trying. Eventually, you either will find a deterrent they really don't like, or the animals will get bored and go elsewhere.

When it comes to people, usually the most effective way to handle them is to offer a tour and fresh produce as it comes ripe. Even the most disapproving neighbor can possibly be swayed by a container of fresh tomatoes and zucchini.

Take a beat. Pest control is a big topic to digest so take your time, reread what we have discussed as often as you need, but an important idea to remember is that pest control is not just a single skirmish. It is an ongoing, low-level fight between you and them. So, plant the plants that will help, attract the insects you can, bribe the neighbors you can, and keep on fighting.

Some years you will have amazing success, while other years the pests will have the upper hand. Don't let this discourage you, for with every plant the pests eat or kill, you have learned something to use on the next one.

Chapter 9:

Herb Your Enthusiasm

Well, here we are. We have covered how to build your raised beds, creating the perfect soil, everything you need to know about water, light, plant care, and good and bad insects. That only leaves us with actually growing plants.

I figure after all the information you have had to absorb and digest so far that we start with simple, big impact plants. I'm talking about herbs. You only need a little to have a big effect, they are hardy, easy plants to grow, and they will fill your garden space with the most enticing aromas.

With today's price of a package of basil seeds at Bunnings, that could grow dozens of full plants, at $1.74 (Bunnings Australia, 2022) and a small bundle of fresh basil at Woolworths costing $3.00 (Woolworths Supermarket, 2022) it makes perfect sense to grow your own.

What could be better than a summer pasta filled with your own fresh tomatoes and basil? Nothing.

So, which herbs should I grow? Which herbs do you like to eat? Herbs are typically a high value item that is best fresh. A perfect choice to grow in your garden. Not only will you save a great deal of money, but they will also be the best, freshest herbs possible, having come from your yard.

The most common herbs to start with are rosemary, coriander, dill, basil, mint, and catnip if you have or like cats. You can add oregano to that list as well if you like the taste of it. These plants are robust, tasty, but more importantly easy to grow. They will forgive any oversights in soil quality, light availability, and of course watering interruptions.

Where to Grow Herbs

We have covered all the details you will need to know about where to place your raised-bed garden, and we will now see how this applies to herbs.

Most herbs will grow quite happily in direct sunlight, in partial sun, and even in the shade. We all have this idea that weeds will grow anywhere, well herbs are basically edible weeds. And this makes them the perfect plants to start your garden off with.

As with most plants, herbs can be started several different ways: from seeds, from store bought seedlings, and from cuttings. If you have a friend that has a huge rosemary plant or thyme bush, then you can snip off a branch—after asking their permission I hope—and wrap the cut area in a wet paper towel.

By keeping this cut damp, you are allowing the branch to continue to absorb moisture, keeping it alive. So, now all you need to do is get back to your garden, make a hole in the soil, add a bit of water, and put in your newly acquired plant. Make sure to keep it well watered for the first couple weeks. By then it should have the beginnings of a root system and be well on the way to a happy and productive life.

Now that we know herbs are easy to start and grow like weeds, that opens up the growing locations beyond your raised beds. What about that slice of dirt beside the driveway? Or the patch in the back lawn where all the grass died off? Or even just in a series of pots along the walk to the house.

If you are planning to grow your herbs in containers, then ideally only one type per pot. If you have a large pot, or a small plant like coriander, then plant several plants per pot, but by keeping each container to a single type of plant, you will make your care and harvesting much simpler.

Herb Gardens

I am pretty confident that once you start growing your own herbs, you will be addicted. Not only do they look beautiful, like the purple flowers of Thai basil, their scent will fill the air on a warm summer's day. And to top it off, they taste fabulous on your food.

We have talked about plant spacing and companion planting for your raised-bed gardening, and that is important to get right to ease your workload and increase your harvest, but when it comes to your herb garden, the rules are somewhat more relaxed.

With most herbs being grown in individual containers, you can arrange them anyway that you fancy. If you like a long, straight row along your fence, then plant that. You can arrange your herbs by size, by color, even alphabetically. Whatever makes you smile. And as you are growing them in containers, then rearranging the layout is a snap when you decide that it is more important to arrange them by the color of the pot or their Latin name.

Does a spiral of aromatic herbs catch your imagination? Well, you can lay out your pots in a spiral, and there you have it! Herbs make both a great garden in themselves—think of your entire raised beds filled with the sweet smell of basil and mint—or accent borders or even solitary pots on the windowsill in your kitchen.

The best way to approach growing herbs is to have fun. Figure out what tastes good to you, what you like the looks or aroma of, and get them growing. More than your raised-bed vegetable garden, your herb garden should make you smile and put you at ease. After all, herbs are the enticing extras you add to your food, the sweet or savory reward for growing all that food.

Now, we cannot not forget about tea. Admittedly, not everyone is a fan of herbal teas. But if you do like herbal tea, then why not grow that as well?

Mint? Put each variety in a separate container and pick the leaves as and when you want a pot. If you are a dedicated mint tea drinker, then you should be pleased to learn that mint is a very vigorous growing plant, as long as you give it lots of water.

Rosehip? Once the rose flowers have passed and the rosehips ripened, pick, dry and make tea. Chamomile, lemon balm, lemongrass, the varieties of herbal teas you can grow are only limited by your imagination, and garden space. Get creative and enjoy. That is what gardening is all about.

Chapter 10:

Growing Guides

So, here you sit, a head full of ideas, plans, and dreams of a fabulous garden. Or perhaps you already have built all your raised beds and found a dozen perfect containers. Either way you are here to find out what is next. How do you care for a cucumber plant, or a basil, or a tomato? Look no further, well actually you will need to turn to the section related to your plant, but figuratively you need go no further.

Most of the advice in the following guides are based on commonsense. And once you have a few years' experience under your belt, you will knowingly or unknowingly have developed your own growing methods for your favorite plants. The nutrient and mineral composition of your soil, the specifics of your water supply, the amount of sunlight, and how much wind annoys you in your garden will all have an effect on how your plants grow. So, as you care for them, month by month, year after year, you will adjust to the needs of your plants, watering as and when they need and composting your soil as you can.

Keeping that in mind, we are going to look at the most common raised bed and container leafy greens, vegetables, and herbs here so you have all the specific details you need in one location. There will be some generalization, like a section on *Brassicas* that will apply to cabbage, broccoli, and cauliflower, as they are all from the same family and have similar growing requirements.

Use these as a point of reference that you can revisit each time you decide to add a new fruit, veggie, or herb to your raised-beds or container garden. Trust me, you won't be content with growing just a few!

Basil

The iconic herb in Italian cooking and the basis for pesto, basil comes in a large number of varieties including the typical sweet Genovese basil, Thai basil, lime basil, and red basil, among many other choices.

When to Plant: Mid spring, once the temperature has warmed up.

When to Harvest: Once the leaves have appeared, then pick as required and remove any flowers to encourage continued leaf growth.

Typical Plant Size: Variable depending on plant, but around 50 centimetres tall and 30 centimetres wide.

Average Yield: Harvest leaves as required.

How to Grow: Plant in well drained and sandy soil. They prefer full sunlight and heat.

How to Plant: From seeds, store bought seedlings, or cuttings.

How to Care: Harvest leaves as required. Ensure soil is well watered and the plant pruned once leaves are removed from stalks.

How to Store: Best if used fresh but can be dehydrated and stored in an airtight container for up to one year.

Common Problems: Aphids love these plants, and basil plants can be subject to downy mildew if not grown in enough heat, enough ventilation, or have been over watered.

Beans

Fancy growing soybeans to make your own delicious edamame from seed? Beans come in a huge number of varieties. The most common ones to plant in your garden are bush, pole, lima, garbanzo, soy, or yard-long, but there are enough different choices to keep you busy for decades trying them all.

When to Plant: Mid spring up to July

When to Harvest: From July through to October once the pods are plump.

Typical Plant Size: Up to 1 metre tall and 20 centimetres across but may grow taller if they are a vining variety.

Average Yield: Approximately two kilo per metre of seeded soil.

How to Grow: Plant in a high quality, moisture holding soil. Provide support for the plants to climb as they grow.

How to Plant: From seeds is the most successful as seedlings are very rare.

How to Care: Plant in a good moisture holding soil, water well, and add compost mid-season if the pods are looking pale.

How to Store: They freeze very well after a quick blanch or can be pickled.

Common Problems: Watch out for slugs.

Brassicas

This covers a wide variety of common plants that include turnips, rutabaga, wasabi and horseradish, kohlrabi, cabbage, collard greens, broccoli, cauliflower, and Brussel sprouts. With such variety there should be at least one of these plants that you will enjoy or want to encourage your little ones to eat more of.

When to Plant: Early spring to late summer depending on your local climate.

When to Harvest: After about 20 weeks and once the head is of sufficient size.

Typical Plant Size: Short but up to 60 centimetres wide.

Average Yield: about 3 kg per metre of planting, or just under 1 kilo per plant.

How to Grow: Plant seeds in well trampled soil

How to Plant: From seeds, as live *Brassica* seedlings are uncommon.

How to Care: They prefer a sunny location with soil rich in compost that is kept moist

How to Store: Best eaten fresh but can be stored in a cool dark place for a few months.

Common Problems: Keep a close eye out for white butterflies and caterpillars.

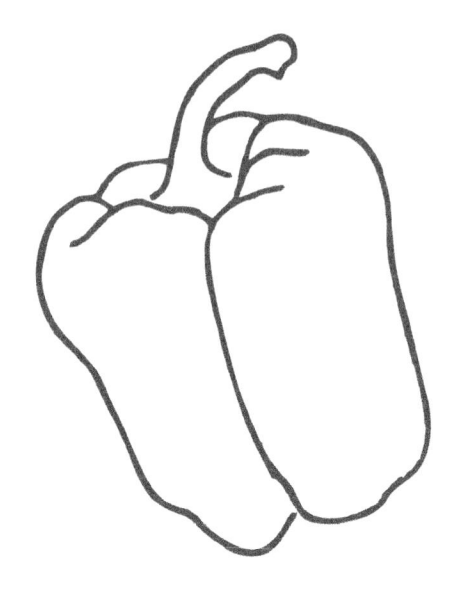

Capsicum

All peppers, from those sweet slices in your salad to those murderously hot peppers that make your eyes sweat, can all be classified as a capsicum. So experiment, find out which ones you like, dislike, and cannot wait to try.

When to Plant: Early spring as soon as temperatures have warmed up.

When to Harvest: Once fruit is of a suitable size and has ripened to desired color.

Typical Plant Size: Usually up to 60 centimetres tall and 30 centimetres wide.

Average Yield: Six to eight per plant.

How to Grow: Start from seeds or live seedlings.

How to Plant: Plant in moist, well-drained soil with good sun exposure.

How to Care: Keep watered and pinch off growing tips once the plant reaches 20 cm tall.

How to Store: Best eaten fresh but can be frozen if necessary.

Common Problems: Look for slugs, grey mould from too much water, and blossom-end rot from insufficient calcium in the soil.

Carrots

Have you ever tried a purple carrot? Or how about a Thumbelina? Now is your chance to learn all about the amazing carrots that never make it into your local grocer.

When to Plant: Early spring through to early fall.

When to Harvest: Early summer through the winter.

Typical Plant Size: Average of 10 cm tall and 5 cm wide.

Average Yield: One kilo per metre of seeding.

How to Grow: From seeds as seedlings will rarely survive transplanting.

How to Plant: Plant in light, well-draining soil, in two week successive plantings.

How to Care: Keep watered. The dense foliage will tend to keep weeds away.

How to Store: Eat fresh, otherwise store in the fridge for a few days, otherwise layer in a box with dry sand and place in a cool location.

Common Problems: Carrot fly. If required, cover the plants with screening.

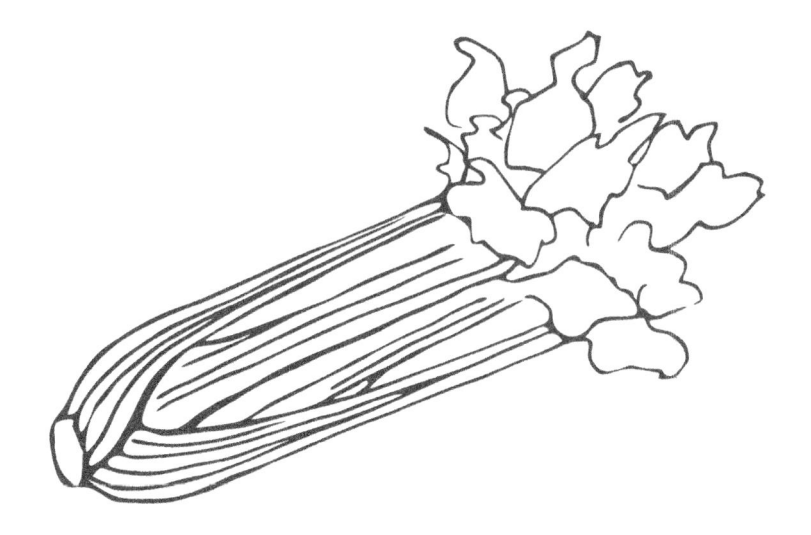

Celery

While not as diverse as carrots or capsicums, celery still has a few choices on hand for you. Try a new one each year. See which taste is your favorite.

When to Plant: Early spring once temperatures are warm enough.

When to Harvest: Late summer and once the stalks are of adequate size.

Typical Plant Size: Approximately 60 centimetres tall and 15 centimetres wide.

Average Yield: One bunch per plant.

How to Grow: From seed as seedlings are rare.

How to Plant: Plant in moist, compost-rich soil in full sunlight.

How to Care: Keep soil moist for the entire growing season.

How to Store: Eat fresh or keep in the fridge for a week or less.

Common Problems: No specific pests, so keep an eye out for typical garden creatures.

Chamomile

In this case, it would be best to stick to the normal chamomile, as it will make the most familiar tasting tea. Save the experimentation for your mint teas.

When to Plant: Year-round.

When to Harvest: Once the flowers are in bloom.

Typical Plant Size: Averaging 60 centimetres tall and 30 centimetres wide.

Average Yield: Several flowers per plant.

How to Grow: From seed.

How to Plant: Plant in a moist compost rich soil, and cover seedlings with only a very thin layer of soil, as they need light to assist with germination.

How to Care: Pick flowers as they appear to encourage plants to produce more flowers.

How to Store: Use fresh for tea or dehydrate and store in an airtight container for up to a year.

Common Problems: Keep watered and local weeds removed.

Citrus

Lemons, limes, and grapefruit to name but a few of the healthy, vitamin-C-filled options bursting with flavour and goodness. Find the ones you like and grow the best fruit you can.

When to Plant: In the spring once it has gotten warm enough.

When to Harvest: Once fruit is of adequate size and color.

Typical Plant Size: Depends on variety but can range from bushes to tall trees.

Average Yield: Depends on variety.

How to Grow: Keep well-watered and in a warm sunny location.

How to Plant: Seeds are slow to start, so ideally from a seedling.

How to Care: Keep well-watered and add compost each year.

How to Store: Depends on variety.

Common Problems: Leaf drop will indicate too much heat and incorrect watering. Sticky leaves are evidence of mealybugs, and damaged leaves usually indicate leafminers are present. Spider mites occasionally select citrus plants and will cover them in fine webs.

Coriander

Now this is divisive: Zesty and sharp to some and like eating soap to others. If you like it, grow it. If not, then use that garden space for some mint to cleanse your palate.

When to Plant: Mid-summer.

When to Harvest: Once plants are of desirable size.

Typical Plant Size: Up t0 20 centimetres tall and 10 centimetres wide.

Average Yield: One plant per seed, harvest as required.

How to Grow: Plant in moist but well-draining soil.

How to Plant: From seeds and succession plant every two weeks to ensure continued supply.

How to Care: Keep well-watered and in bright sunlight.

How to Store: Use fresh but can be dehydrated and stored in airtight container for a year.

Common Problems: Look out for slugs and snails.

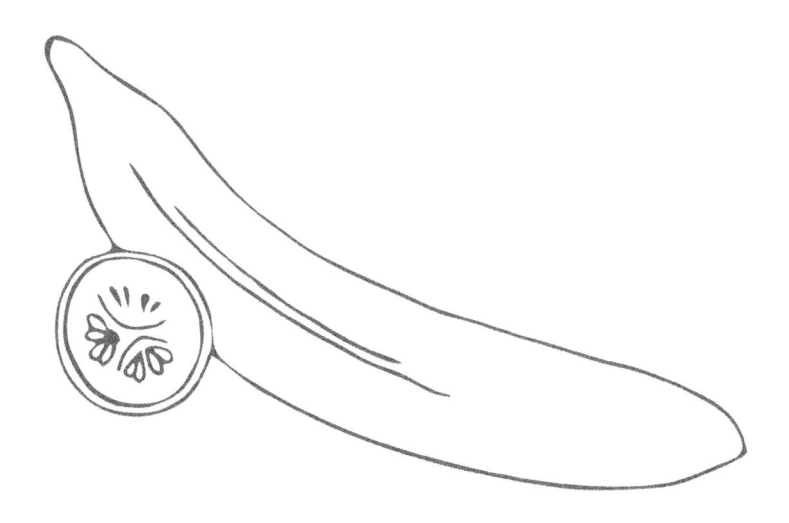

Cucumbers

Now, cucumbers have many uses: in sandwiches, on burgers, and as pickles. There are more types of cucumbers than you can imagine. So, take your time at the garden store next time you are there and learn about the different cucumber seeds they offer. I am sure you will be surprised at the variety on hand.

When to Plant: Early spring.

When to Harvest: Once fruit is of desired size.

Typical Plant Size: Usually around 60 centimetres tall and 30 centimetres wide, unless the variety is not a bush but is a creeping vine.

Average Yield: Multiple per plant.

How to Grow: Plant seeds in moist, compost-rich soil. Provide support if needed.

How to Plant: From seeds as seedlings are rare and do not survive well.

How to Care: Keep well-watered and ensure flowers are pollinated if the plant is not a self-pollinating variety.

How to Store: Eat fresh but can be pickled.

Common Problems: Aphids love these plants, as do whiteflies and spider mites. Over watering may cause powdery mildew as well.

Figs

Blue province, Conadria, excel, green ischia, white ischia, Tena, and Flanders. Sounds like a list of coffee beans from your local cafe, but it is in fact the common types of figs. Have you tasted them all? I have not. So why not try and grow them? Your new favorite food might be waiting right here for you to discover.

When to Plant: Late fall

When to Harvest: Once fruit is of adequate size and color, there may be a drop of sugar at the bottom of each fruit.

Typical Plant Size: Up to three metres tall and four metres wide.

Average Yield: In the range of 50 per tree.

How to Grow: Plant in a warm, sheltered location in full sunshine.

How to Plant: From seed will be slow. Best if you can find a seedling of the variety you desire.

How to Care: Keep well-watered and add compost every year.

How to Store: Best eaten fresh but can be dried and stored in a cool dry location for a few weeks.

Common Problems: Birds and most animals like figs. Wasps will come to fallen fruit, and unexpected leaf drop may indicate insufficient watering.

Kale

Big, green healthy leaves, kinda hard to chew. We all know this about kale, but once you get over the stigma of it, it is a great plant. Kale salads last more than an hour before going soggy, kale chips… Well, they are glorious. Take some time and get to know kale. It is worth the effort.

When to Plant: Early spring.

When to Harvest: Once leaves are of desired size.

Typical Plant Size: Roughly 60 centimetres both tall and wide.

Average Yield: Many leaves per plant.

How to Grow: Plant in moist, well-drained soil in full sunlight, but will tolerate some shade.

How to Plant: From seeds as seedlings are very rare.

How to Care: Add compost to soil before planting. Remove any flowers to promote leaf growth. Keep soil moist.

How to Store: Use fresh but can be blanched and frozen.

Common Problems: Very few, only some hungry birds.

Leeks

They are good in potato soup. But what else? Here is your chance to grow some and find out! I am sure you will be pleasantly surprised.

When to Plant: Late spring to early summer.

When to Harvest: Late summer into autumn.

Typical Plant Size: Roughly 30 centimetres tall and 10 centimetres wide.

Average Yield: One per plant.

How to Grow: Start seeds inside in pots and transplant to the garden once temperature has increased and seedlings are well established.

How to Plant: From seeds as seedlings are rare to find.

How to Care: Keep well-watered and weeded.

How to Store: Use fresh or store in the fridge for a couple of weeks.

Common Problems: Leaf moth, leaf miners, and leek rust may be visible during the growing season.

Lettuce

Iceberg, romaine, red leaf, purple leaf, I could go on. There seems to be a new type of lettuce out each month. But by growing your own, you get to decide what variety, and how you like your salads. Soft tender new shoots filled with the sweetness of spring, or hardier, full-flavoured leaves redolent with summer's good weather. So many choices for you to try.

When to Plant: Early spring and succession planting every week.

When to Harvest: Once the plant is of desired size, usually after 6 weeks.

Typical Plant Size: Usually about 15 centimetres tall and wide, but that will change with different varieties.

Average Yield: One head per plant.

How to Grow: Plant seeds in moist, composted soil.

How to Plant: From seed.

How to Care: Keep well-watered to reduce tendency to bolt, after which the lettuce will be bitter.

How to Store: Eat fresh otherwise store in the fridge for a week or less.

Common Problems: Slugs and snails love a good lettuce feed.

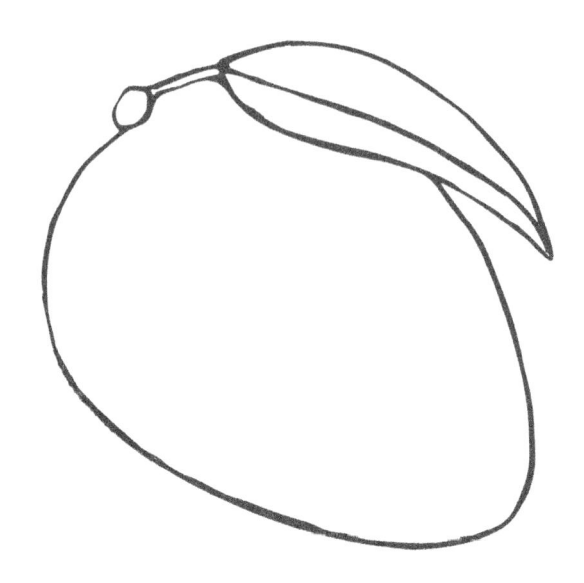

Mangoes

What else can you say about the king of fruit? Enjoy some in your brekky smoothie, or pop into your Thermomix to whip up a delectable and healthy ice cream.

Plant some and enjoy it.

When to Plant: Year-round.

When to Harvest: Once the fruit skin has turned yellow, orange, or red, usually 150 days after flowering.

Typical Plant Size: Up to 10 metres tall and 5 metres in width.

Average Yield: Many fruits per tree.

How to Grow: Plant in well-composted soil, with good drainage and full sunlight.

How to Plant: From seed is very slow so find a small tree in the variety you want to grow.

How to Care: Keep well-watered and fertilize yearly.

How to Store: Eat fresh but can be frozen or dried.

Common Problems: Trees are susceptible to fruit flies and fungal diseases if not adequately ventilated.

Mint

Spearmint, chocolate, ginger, apple, the list of types of mint is seemingly endless. If you like mint teas, then this is your chance to make that truly perfect pot of tea. Perhaps it is ginger mint with a hint of apple? Or spearmint with equal parts Moroccan and Egyptian? Let your tastebuds guide you.

When to Plant: Commonly planted between March and April but can also be planted in autumn if the local winter is mild enough.

When to Harvest: Once leaves have appeared, then pick as required.

Typical Plant Size: Up to one metre in both width and height, but roots will travel, and it is recommended that mint be grown in a large container to control the spread.

Average Yield: As required.

How to Grow: From germinated seeds, live seedlings, or cutting from existing plants.

How to Plant: Pot in well-draining soil

How to Care: Harvest leaves as needed. Let some stalks flower to attract pollinators, and once the season is over, trim the plant near to the soil and let it overwinter. Mint will regrow every year if well looked after.

How to Store: Use fresh, if possible, but leaves can be dehydrated and kept in an airtight container for up to one year.

Common Problems: Stalks that look swollen with orange spots are an indication of mint rust. If found, then the plant should be removed and disposed of.

Onions

Sweet, white, red. Pretty simple on the surface, but a home-grown onion has subtleties of taste you can't imagine, until you have tried one. Go and grow some, I'll wait to hear what you think.

When to Plant: Early spring and early fall.

When to Harvest: Early summer for fall planting and early fall for spring planting.

Typical Plant Size: roughly 10 centimetres wide and up to 30 centimetres tall.

Average Yield: Ten large onions per metre of seeded soil.

How to Grow: Seeds are very slow. Choose onion sets of the variety you want to grow.

How to Plant: Moist, compost-rich soil.

How to Care: Keep well-watered and weed free.

How to Store: Use fresh or hang from stalks in a cool dark location until needed.

Common Problems: Cover to reduce bird damage. Yellow foliage may indicate onion fly larvae and grey mould near the soil may occur when overwatered.

Parsley

Perhaps the perfect accompaniment? Easy to grow and abundant. Make sure you never run out.

When to Plant: Early spring.

When to Harvest: Late summer and when leaves are of adequate size.

Typical Plant Size: Around 45 centimetres tall and 30 centimetres wide.

Average Yield: Many leaves per plant.

How to Grow: Plant in moist, well-drained soil in sun to partial shade.

How to Plant: From seeds.

How to Care: Keep well-watered and add compost mid-season.

How to Store: Use fresh but can be dehydrated and stored for up to a year.

Common Problems: The usual suspects of snails and slugs but also carrot fly can be bothersome.

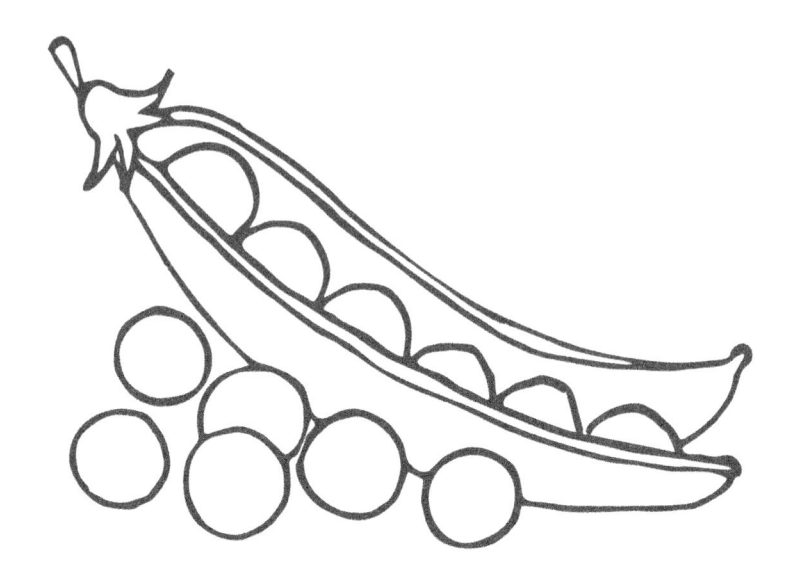

Peas

Once the bad boy on your childhood dinner plate, peas have been reborn in fusion cooking and as a healthy snack. Keep on trend, find your ideal pea.

When to Plant: Pretty much year-round.

When to Harvest: Once the pods have filled in and the peas inside are plump.

Typical Plant Size: Only about 10 centimetres wide but will climb up to 2 metres.

Average Yield: One kilo of peas per seeded metre of soil.

How to Grow: Plant in good, composted soil.

How to Plant: From seeds.

How to Care: Keep well-watered and supported as the plant grows.

How to Store: Use fresh or can be blanched and frozen.

Common Problems: Again, look out for slugs.

Potatoes

Mashed, boiled, or chopped into wedges and roasted to perfection ready to dip into your sweet chilli sauce? How do you like your spuds? There is one that is perfect for you.

When to Plant: Early spring.

When to Harvest: Once the foliage has died back.

Typical Plant Size: About 60 centimetres both tall and wide.

Average Yield: Three kilos of potatoes per seeded metre of soil.

How to Grow: Plant seed potatoes in moist well composted soil.

How to Plant: From seed potatoes.

How to Care: Keep watered and as the plant grows, pile up dirt around the stalk to provide more depth for tubers to grow.

How to Store: Use fresh or store in a cool dark location for up to six months.

Common Problems: Again, for the slugs but also potato blight fungus which will cause the tubers to rot. Rotate potato growing location each year.

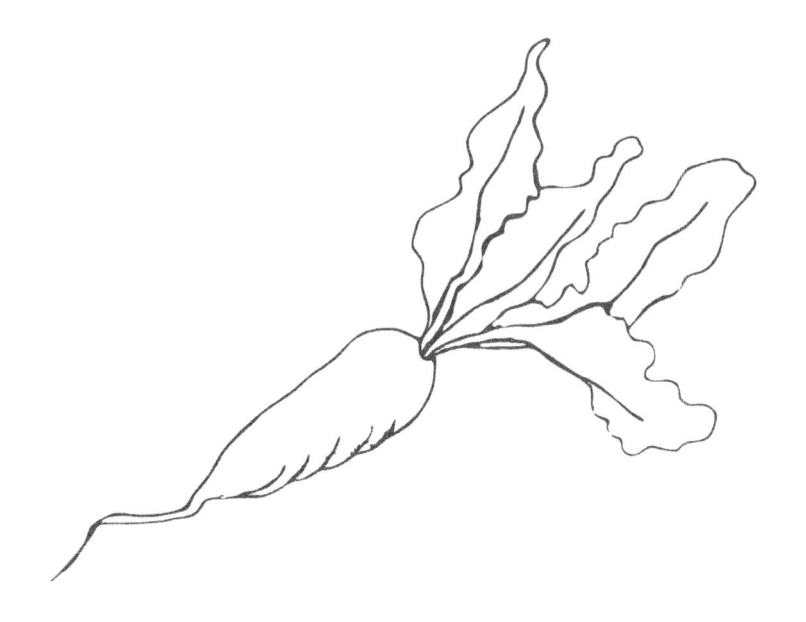

Radishes

Tiny mouthfuls of fire and ice. A perfect accent to a summer salad or fiery snack to get you through the afternoon.

When to Plant: Early spring and then succession planted every week.

When to Harvest: Within three to four weeks of planting.

Typical Plant Size: About 10 centimetres tall and 5 centimetres wide.

Average Yield: One bulb per plant.

How to Grow: Seed in fine, well-drained soil.

How to Plant: From seeds.

How to Care: Keep well-watered and weed free. Thin as needed.

How to Store: Use fresh.

Common Problems: Our old friends, the snails and slugs.

Spinach

Not only Popeye's best friend but an iron-rich booster to your salads, smoothies, and sandwiches.

When to Plant: Early spring with succession planting every two weeks.

When to Harvest: Once leaves are of desired size.

Typical Plant Size: About 15 centimetres tall and 10 centimetres wide.

Average Yield: Many leaves per plant.

How to Grow: Plant seeds in moist, composted soil in partial shade.

How to Plant: From seeds.

How to Care: Keep well-watered and weeded.

How to Store: Use fresh but can be frozen.

Common Problems: Again, with the snails and slugs.

Strawberries

Strawberries are a great addition to summery cocktails to add that sweet, floral flavour. Muddle them, turn them into strawberry simple syrup, or infuse them into vodka or sangria. Or if your kids are anything like mine, freshly chopped over their daily Weetbix goes down a treat.

When to Plant: Early spring with weekly succession planting.

When to Harvest: Once berries are plump and red.

Typical Plant Size: Around 30 centimetres both wide and tall.

Average Yield: Typically, half a kilo per plant.

How to Grow: Well-composted, moist soil in a sunny location.

How to Plant: From seedlings.

How to Care: Keep well-watered and weeded and cover to deter bird damage.

How to Store: Use fresh but can be frozen.

Common Problems: Yet again, with snails and slugs, but also powdery mildew, and grey mould.

Sweet Potatoes

The perfect accompaniment for healthy kids' dinners, or a guilt-free alternative to french fries. Why not have an abundance ready to use as you please?

When to Plant: Early spring.

When to Harvest: Once foliage begins to die back, usually 16 weeks after planting.

Typical Plant Size: Between 20 and 30 centimetres tall but also may vine.

Average Yield: Potentially many tubers per plant.

How to Grow: Plant slips on composted, well-draining soil in bright sun.

How to Plant: From slips.

How to Care: Keep well-watered.

How to Store: Use fresh, cure in the sun for several hours a day for about 10 days and then store in a cool dark location for up to six months.

Common Problems: Red spider mite. Use pressure water to remove.

Tomatoes

And tomatoes. They are a mainstay in your summer salads, your salsa, and pastas. Life would be very boring without tomatoes. So, if you are looking for a good sauce, grow Romas. A perfect round slice on your burger or sandwich, try a beefsteak. Now, when was the last time you had black tomatoes? Or yellow ones? Grow them and prepare to be amazed.

When to Plant: Early spring.

When to Harvest: Last summer or when fruit is desired size and ripe.

Typical Plant Size: Around 40 centimetres tall and wide unless the plant is of a vining variety.

Average Yield: About two and a half kilo per plant.

How to Grow: Plant in moist, composted soil and keep watered. Support as needed.

How to Plant: From seeds or seedlings.

How to Care: Keep supported and well-watered, especially into the later part of the season.

How to Store: Use fresh but can be canned, dried, or frozen.

Common Problems: Whitefly larvae and tomato blight can be common. If your soil is low on calcium, you will also encounter blossom end blight.

Sow the Seeds for Someone Else

Now that you realize just how easy it is to grow your own food, I'm sure you're raring to go… but before you do, bear in mind that you're in the perfect position to help a fellow gardener.

Simply by leaving your honest opinion of this book on Amazon, you'll show new readers where they can find the same guidance that has inspired you.

LEAVE A REVIEW!

Thank you for your support. Raised bed gardening has so much to offer – and I want to make sure as many people have access to it as possible.

Conclusion

I can only imagine that you are as anxious as I was to get out and start creating your own raised-bed or container gardens, so I will only keep you a few minutes longer. I wanted to go over what we have covered, on the off chance there is something you missed or needed to review.

With the skyrocketing price of food—and I am not just talking about organic, healthy food stocking the shelves of that boutique grocer down the road, but even the low-quality fast-food endemic to our modern diet has gotten expensive—there is no better time than now to grow your own food.

It doesn't matter if you grew up in a farming family and just need a refresher or have never grown anything in your life. Together, we have walked step by step through the entire process from creating your garden space, figuring out and preparing your soil, choosing plants, and learning how to look after them until they are ready to be harvested. We will leave all those amazing dinner recipes to you and your Pinterest board.

The next way to save money is to make your own fertilizer, known as compost. Seeing as you have already paid for the nutrients in your food scraps, it only makes sense to recycle them into next year's produce. Not only does this create more produce next year, which saves you money, you are reusing your food waste to create compost, which also saves you having to buy an expensive, commercial fertilizer. There is a beautiful symmetry with your leftovers fertilizing next year's garden.

And what about your seeds? Sure, grocery store seedlings are a quick and simple way to start your plants, and I would recommend purchasing these for new gardeners. But after the first year of growing, you can harvest the seeds from those plants as long as you let one of each type go all the way to seed, or not harvest the fruit prematurely. Once you have these seeds dried, you can store them and germinate them in the spring, saving you the cost of either new seed packages or live seedlings.

After the first year, you will likely not have to buy seeds ever again, unless you want to add a new vegetable, fruit, or berry choice to your garden. Another way to save some money is to grow your plants from cuttings of healthy growing plants. If you have a gorgeous tomato plant that grows amazing tasting tomatoes, and your friend has a cucumber plant that just thrives, trade cuttings. All you need is a sharp knife, or a good pair of scissors, and some wet paper towel. Cut a section off your plant, making sure there are several leaves and ideally a branching section above your cut. Once the piece is separated from the main plant, quickly wrap it in the wet paper towel. For the cutting to grow new roots, you need to keep the cut surface damp until you can plant it when you get home. So, for only the cost of a couple paper towel sheets, both you and your friend get to share your love of gardening and add to your ranges of veggies you have growing. The possibilities are only limited to your imagination and creativity and how many of your friends have plants.

Water. Either from your city supply or harvested rainwater. Rainwater can be collected in anything that holds water: a wheelbarrow, a bucket, or even a tarp. And your plants will thank you for the clean, healthy water.

I think you will have to admit that now you know the fundamentals of growing your own food, that is it much simpler than you were expecting. Remember you do not have to spend very much money to get started growing your own food, the money you do spend will be a very lucrative investment for many years of produce, and your savings will begin the first time you pick that juicy plump tomato for a bruschetta or chop up a newly ripened cucumber for your salad. And you will continue to save money for as long as you grow, eat, and store the produce from your garden.

So, before you head out and spend all sorts of money on building or purchasing new raised beds, just remember that they do not need to be fancy. All they need to do is hold dirt. And having holes in the bottom will be very helpful. So, look around. Take some time to look through your storage area, or your sister's back shed, or your friend's garage. I expect you will find something that can be pressed into service to create your first raised-bed garden for little or no money.

We have touched on so many topics here that I feel it would be a waste of your gardening time to simply repeat it all, so will leave you here with a few parting thoughts.

Gardening is a fun and rewarding pastime that will fundamentally change your view of food and food security as long as you live. Everyone, even those of you that can never manage to keep any plants alive or have never even tried, can grow your own food. As you now know, the steps are few and simple, so do not let your confidence waver. You can do this. And finally, there is no better way to connect with your food, your friends and family, and save money while improving the quality of what you eat.

Just imagine the amount of savings you can accumulate over the years as you learn to grow, eat and store the delicious yields right from your own backyard. The possibilities are endless—but before you get started on Step 1, please leave a review on Amazon if you enjoyed this book. Happy gardening!

References

About pollinators. (2017, May 28). *Pollinator.org*. https://www.pollinator.org/pollinators

ATGadmin. (2013). *Summer herb, fruit & vegies planting guide by temperate zones*. About the Garden Magazine. https://www.aboutthegarden.com.au/summer-herb-fruit-vegetable-planting-guide-by-temperate-zone/

Autumn herb, fruit & vegies planting guide by temperate zones. (n.d.). About the Garden Magazine. Retrieved September 21, 2022, from https://www.aboutthegarden.com.au/autumn-flower-herb-fruit-vegetable-planting-guide-by-temperate-zone/

Beck, A. (2022, May 14). *Beginner Vegetable Gardening Made Easy*. Better Homes & Gardens; Better Homes & Gardens. https://www.bhg.com/gardening/vegetable/vegetables/planning-your-first-vegetable-garden/

Beneficial Insect Identification Guides. (n.d.). Www.growveg.com.au. Retrieved September 22, 2022, from https://www.growveg.com.au/beneficial-insects/australia-and-nz/

Bradbury, K. (2010, November 12). *Crop Rotation for Growing Vegetables.* GrowVeg. https://www.growveg.com.au/guides/crop-rotation-for-growing-vegetables/

Bunnings Australia. (2022). Search Results. Bunnings.com.au. https://www.bunnings.com.au/search/products?q=basil%20seeds&sort=BoostOrder&page=1

Christina Aguilera (Ft. Redman) – *Dirrty.* (n.d.). Genius.com. Retrieved September 22, 2022, from https://genius.com/Christina-aguilera-dirrty-lyrics

Deutsh, S. (2018, September 27). *How To Design Your Backyard Vegetable Patch* | ModularWalls. Modularwalls.com.au. https://modularwalls.com.au/blog/how-to-backyard-vegetable-patch/

Dore, J. (2010, November 19). *Keeping Cats off Vegetable Beds.* GrowVeg. https://www.growveg.com.au/guides/keeping-cats-off-vegetable-beds/

Homemade Seed Mats or Seed Tapes. (2014, April 20). Grow a Good Life. https://growagoodlife.com/homemade-seed-mats/

How to Build a Square Foot Garden. (2021, February 6). Grow a Good Life. https://growagoodlife.com/assembling-the-sfg/

How to grow mint. (2020, March 14). BBC Gardeners' World Magazine. https://www.gardenersworld.com/how-to/grow-plants/how-to-grow-mint/

Jimerson, D. (2022, August 5). *10 Vegetable Gardening Mistakes Even Good Gardeners Make.* Better Homes & Gardens. https://www.bhg.com/gardening/vegetable/vegetables/10-vegetable-gardening-mistakes-even-good-gardeners-make/

Kelly, C. (2022, June 2). *Why does this iceberg lettuce cost $11.99 and how long will Australia's high vegetable prices last?* The Guardian. https://www.theguardian.com/food/2022/jun/03/why-does-this-iceberg-lettuce-cost-1199-and-how-long-will-australias-high-vegetable-prices-last

Lamp'l, J. (2018, March 15). *Raised Bed Gardening | Best Soil Recipe| joe gardener®*. Joe Gardener® | Organic Gardening like a Pro. https://joegardener.com/podcast/raised-bed-gardening-pt-2/

Life, F. G. (2017, October 31). *Beneficial insects in Australia | top 6 you should know*. Family Garden Life. https://familygardenlife.com/top-benefical-insects-australia/

Neveln, V. (2022, July 21). *Follow These Tips for a Healthy Organic Veggie Garden*. Better Homes & Gardens. https://www.bhg.com/gardening/vegetable/vegetables/tips-for-growing-an-organic-vegetable-garden/

Poindexter, J. (2018, March 16). *19 Vegetable Garden Care & Maintenance Tips for a Successful Harvest*. MorningChores. https://morningchores.com/vegetable-garden-care/

Reilly, K. (2022, April 18). *8 Common Raised Garden Mistakes You Might Be Making*. Better Homes & Gardens. https://www.bhg.com/gardening/how-to-garden/raised-bed-garden-mistakes/

Spring Herb, Fruit & Vegies Planting Guide By Regional Zones. (n.d.). About the Garden Magazine. Retrieved September 21, 2022, from https://www.aboutthegarden.com.au/spring-herb-fruit-vegies-planting-guide-by-regional-zones/

theminismallholder. (2021, April 17). *Crops That Thrive In Soggy, Wet Soil*. Homegrown Herb Garden.

https://homegrownherbgarden.com/2021/04/17/crops-that-thrive-in-soggy-wet-soil/

The 29 Best Charlie Sheen Quotes: The Definitive List. (2011, March 1). Funny or Die. https://funnyordie.com/2011/03/01/65611/the-29-best-charlie-sheen-quotes-the-definitive-list/

10 Steps to Starting Seedlings Indoors. (2016, January 18). Grow a Good Life. https://growagoodlife.com/starting-seedlings-indoors/

29 Common Garden Pests in Australia and How to Get Rid of Them - Fantastic Gardeners Melbourne. (2017, February 22). Fantastic Gardeners Blog. https://blog.fantasticgardenersmelbourne.com.au/common-garden-pests-australia/

Top 13 pollination quotes. (n.d.). *A-Z Quotes.* https://www.azquotes.com/quotes/topics/pollination.html

Vanheems, B. (2015, June 19). *Watering Your Vegetable Garden: How to Water Plants for Healthier Growth.* GrowVeg. https://www.growveg.com.au/guides/watering-your-vegetable-garden-how-to-water-plants-for-healthier-growth/

Vanheems, B. (2016a, June 24). *How to Make a Self-Watering Plant Pot.* GrowVeg. https://www.growveg.com.au/guides/how-to-make-a-self-watering-plant-pot/

Vanheems, B. (2016b, October 14). *Companion Planting: Why Vegetables Need Friends.* GrowVeg. https://www.growveg.com.au/guides/companion-planting-why-vegetables-need-friends/

Vanheems, B. (2017, January 13). *Companion Planting Made Easy.* GrowVeg.

https://www.growveg.com.au/guides/companion-planting-made-easy/

Vanheems, B. (2018, February 23). *How to Make the Best Potting Mix for Starting Seeds.* GrowVeg. https://www.growveg.com.au/guides/how-to-make-the-best-potting-mix-for-starting-seeds/

Vanheems, B. (2019, April 11). *5 Best Crops for Your Edible Container Garden.* GrowVeg. https://www.growveg.com.au/guides/5-best-crops-for-your-edible-container-garden/

Vanheems, B. (2021, August 7). *Start a Herb Garden on a Budget.* GrowVeg. https://www.growveg.com.au/guides/start-a-herb-garden-on-a-budget/

Williamson, L. (2020, October 20). *Mango Trees: How to Grow a Mango Tree.* Better Homes and Gardens. https://www.bhg.com.au/mango-trees-how-to-grow-a-mango-tree

Winter Herb, Fruit & Vegies Planting Guide By Regional Zones. (n.d.). About the Garden Magazine. Retrieved September 21, 2022, from https://www.aboutthegarden.com.au/winter-herb-fruit-vegies-planting-guide-by-regional-zones/

Woolworths Supermarket. (n.d.). Search Results. Www.woolworths.com.au. Retrieved September 24, 2022, from https://www.woolworths.com.au/shop/search/products?searchTerm=Basil

Wytmans, K. (2021, March 25). *Herb Gardening Can Save Home Cooks a Ton of Money—Here's How.* Better Homes & Gardens. https://www.bhg.com/gardening/vegetable/herb-garden-cooking-cut-costs/

Printed in Great Britain
by Amazon